PLANTS & GARDENS

BROOKLYN BOTANIC GARDEN RECORD

R O S E S

THIS HANDBOOK IS A REVISED EDITION OF PLANTS & GARDENS, VOL. 36, No. 1

HANDBOOK # 92

FOREWORD

D.S. STUMP

Most of my working life, over thirty-five years, has been spent in the nursery industry with two firms, both specializing in the hybridizing and marketing of roses. It has been a rewarding and satisfying experience.

Growing roses is the kind of business where friendships are formed that are different and closer than those experienced in most industries. From among those many friends were selected the authors whose writings have made this revised Handbook possible. I thank them all.

To say that very early I fell in love with roses is not an overstatement. My formal training was in the area of advertising and graphic arts, and my entry into the nursery industry opened a whole new world ... the fascinating world of plants—plant production and marketing, plant breeding and evaluation, plant identification and nomenclature. There was much to learn and each bit of knowledge gained led to even more to be learned. This wonderful life of learning continues even now.

But it was the ROSE, the most universally used and loved ornamental plant, that captured me completely. Although I was associated with plant breeding of various ornamentals and fruit trees, working with roses became my prime engagement—and one could not have asked for or enjoyed more this happy and fruitful "marriage."

One of my first jobs was to count rose plants in the nursery and make an estimate of the crop grade for the coming season. It was necessary to quickly learn variety identification. Color and form of the flower are not always reliable because of the variability that occurs, depending on the growing locality. Herb Swim taught me to learn the distinction of foliage, arrangement of thorns, and other characteristics of the plant which are more uniform indicators so one would not rely solely on color and form for identification.

It was also with Herb Swim, along with Awdry Armstrong, that I was initiated into the marvelous world of evaluating new rose seedlings. Words are not adequate to express the feeling that comes when one sees a new rose for the first time. In those days, all new seedlings were transplanted from the germination flat to small clay pots and then transplanted to the nursery row, so that when first seen in bloom, we were looking at the original seedling.

I have no record of how many thousands of seedlings I've looked at or how many notes I have written over the years—it would be in the hundreds of thousands. But out of all those roses, I'd

D.S. STUMP, *President of Jackson & Perkins Co. in Medford, Oregon, one of the worlds's leading rose nurseries, is Guest Editor of this Handbook.*

PLANTS & GARDENS

BROOKLYN BOTANIC GARDEN RECORD

ROSES

1990

Brooklyn Botanic Garden

STAFF FOR THE ORIGINAL EDITION:

D.S. STUMP, GUEST EDITOR

FREDERICK MCGOURTY, JR., EDITOR

STAFF FOR THE REVISED EDITION:

BARBARA B. PESCH, DIRECTOR OF PUBLICATIONS

JANET MARINELLI, ASSOCIATE EDITOR

AND THE EDITORIAL COMMITTEE OF THE BROOKLYN BOTANIC GARDEN

BEKKA LINDSTROM, ART DIRECTOR

JUDITH D. ZUK, PRESIDENT, BROOKLYN BOTANIC GARDEN

ELIZABETH SCHOLTZ, DIRECTOR EMERITUS, BROOKLYN BOTANIC GARDEN

STEPHEN K-M. TIM, VICE PRESIDENT, SCIENCE & PUBLICATIONS

COVER PHOTOGRAPH OF BBG'S CRANFORD ROSE GARDEN BY ELVIN MCDONALD
PHOTOGRAPHS BY ELVIN MCDONALD, EXCEPT WHERE NOTED

guess that not over several hundred have ever been marketed or seen by those of you who will read and use this Handbook.

There is nothing quite as exciting, at least to me, as seeing for the very first time an outstanding bloom on a new seedling. It is a stimulating mental experience. A multitude of questions immediately crosses the mind. Is it distinctive? Is it a new or different color? Is the plant vigorous? Is it reasonably disease-free? And on and on. Oh, and is it fragrant?

In walking the seedling fields, a grower finds that his eye is always attracted by color. I have a habit of snapping a bloom off when I'm attracted by its color and I may glance at its form as the bloom is on the way to my nose to test for fragrance. I remember walking a seedling field one day with several notable rose breeders, among whom was Fred Howard. Fred was walking down the rows of seedlings, snapping off blooms, smelling them and throwing them on the ground, and finally saying, "You young rose breeders don't know how to breed for fragrance."

There are many who believe that there are not as many fragrant roses being introduced today as in the past, but my research does not support that. While breeding for fragrance is a most elusive task, there are just as many fragrant roses introduced now as there were fifty years ago.

In looking back over the years, it is easy to see the improvements that rose breeders have made to the rose. There have been new colors combined with better form, flowers that have better substance, are less influenced by the vagaries of weather, and are longer lasting on the plant or when cut.

The greatest improvement has been in plant vigor and, consequently, greater flower production. Varieties that we were growing when I first counted them in the field would not get a second look in our seedling fields today. Varieties that were deficient in vigor have simply passed out of commerce.

As I write this, it is autumn and in a few weeks we will be looking at our seedlings for the last time this year. We will be reviewing final selection of a limited number of seedlings and making decisions on their introduction four or five years hence. The notes will be reviewed (many of them may go back four or five years) and after much discussion the die will be cast—to go ahead or discard.

But the next spring the process starts anew. We will be seeing a new rose for the first time in the nursery row, and perhaps we'll see the first perfect rose. Doubtful, yes, but then, "Man's reach must be greater than his grasp or what's a heaven for?"

Helping to put this Handbook together has been interesting and enjoyable. The authors might have many differing opinions, but all have one thing in common—love of the rose. I hope you find the articles they have contributed to be interesting and useful. Further, it is the hope of all of us that your use of this Handbook will encourage you to plant and grow roses, and that you'll share our love of this most useful and beautiful of all ornamental plants. ❧

HOW ROSES ARE CLASSIFIED

R. J. HUTTON

The botanical group of plants we call roses is exceedingly large and complicated. There have been one hundred fifty recognized and described species of roses found throughout the northern hemisphere from *Rosa blanda* of northern Canada to *Rosa clinophylla* of the tropics. Over twelve thousand kinds of roses are listed in *Modern Roses 7* published in 1969. A form of classification of the many rose types is necessary to group them accordingly to similar characteristics. Unfortunately, there is not full agreement as to what these groups should be and how they should be defined. The problem of classification of roses is due to their diversity, popularity, wide distribution and complex crossbreeding.

Those who have an interest in classifying roses include: the scientific community for whom botanical classification is an all-important tool; the hobbyist who grows roses for exhibition in competitive rose shows, to whom competitive classes must be clearly defined; and the gardening public who buy most of the roses grown, sold and enjoyed in the United States and throughout the world.

R.J. HUTTON *is President of The Conard-Pyle Co. in West Grove, Pennsylvania.*

It is for the gardening public that this is written as guidance and clarification.

A system of classification is possible by observing growth characteristics and by cataloging the uses which take best advantage of these growth characteristics. However, when a group of plants is so highly crossbred as roses, it is only natural that lines are crossed and gradations are no longer clear cut. This leads to occasional arbitrary decisions. Also, it is not unusual for a variety to display a different habit of growth in the cool New England air than it does in the hot, dry Southwest. What may be a well-defined grandiflora in a hybridizer's California test fields might grow more like a hybrid tea along the Gulf Coast and a floribunda along the Canadian border.

The uses we make of roses is determined primarily by the growth habit of the plants and their flowering characteristics, as well as some differences such as winter hardiness which are outwardly less visible. This brings us to our first broad functional classification:

INDOOR ROSES: A small but increasingly important group made up of those especially bred for the fresh-flower market and as flowering pot plants. Their physical characteristics overlap with the out-

Roses Classed by Growth Characteristics & Most Common Usage

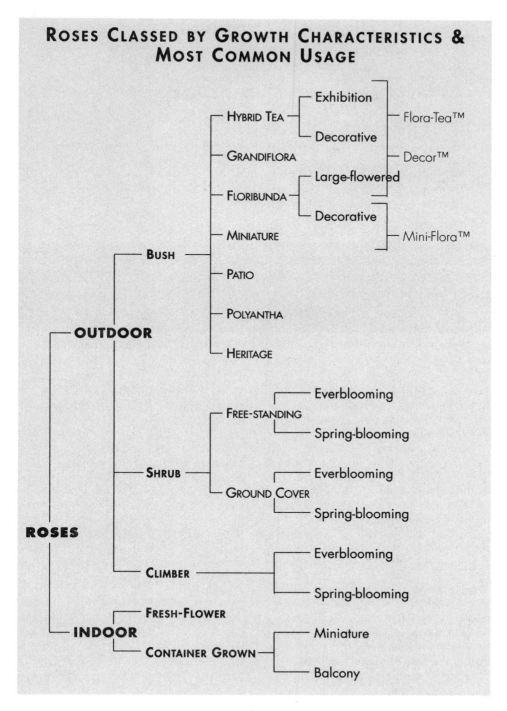

- **OUTDOOR**
  - **BUSH**
    - **HYBRID TEA**
      - Exhibition — Flora-Tea™
      - Decorative
    - **GRANDIFLORA** — Decor™
    - **FLORIBUNDA**
      - Large-flowered
      - Decorative — Mini-Flora™
    - **MINIATURE**
    - **PATIO**
    - **POLYANTHA**
    - **HERITAGE**
  - **SHRUB**
    - **FREE-STANDING**
      - Everblooming
      - Spring-blooming
    - **GROUND COVER**
      - Everblooming
      - Spring-blooming
  - **CLIMBER**
    - Everblooming
    - Spring-blooming
- **INDOOR**
  - **FRESH-FLOWER**
  - **CONTAINER GROWN**
    - Miniature
    - Balcony

- **ROSES**

Hybrid tea 'Headliner', a 1986 All-America Rose Selection winner.

door roses, but their genetic makeup is such that they grow and flower under the controlled environment of greenhouses and adapt to brightly lit homes or offices.

OUTDOOR ROSES: Here we have the great majority of types and sizes of both plant and flower. Outdoor roses include all the garden types and natural species and comprise 99.9 percent of the different roses known and grown.

Next we can establish broad classifications of outdoor roses. Let's look at three groups separated by general growth characteristics:

BUSH ROSES: Self-supporting, upright growing plants bearing flowers primarily on the top of the plant; plant height ranges from a few inches to five or six feet under average growing conditions in most of the United States.

CLIMBING ROSES: Those of exceptional vigor, producing long canes which require support. These may range from five feet to twenty feet or more depending on the kind and how they are supported and maintained.

SHRUB AND GROUND COVER ROSES: Shrubs are broad, upright plants whose canes are self-supporting but tend to arch in graceful forms. Ground cover roses are prostrate plants or those which have a slightly arched growth then trail along the ground. Both usually have flowers borne in trusses at the ends of the canes and from branches along the canes.

Bush Roses

Of the three groups the most commonly used and by far the best known are the bush roses. They break down into four important categories: hybrid tea, grandiflora, floribunda and miniature. In

8

'New Dawn', an everblooming climber.

'Queen Elizabeth', a grandiflora and AARS winner in 1955.

addition, and of less importance, are polyantha, patio roses, heritage (old) roses and commercial trademarks such as Flora-Tea, Mini-Flora and Decor roses.

HYBRID TEAS: Here we have the aristocrats of rosedom, the most popular type of roses in America today. They feature attractive buds and relatively large flowers, well-formed and symmetrical. The plants are vigorous enough to provide more-or-less continuous bloom. In general they grow from 2 1/2 to five feet tall and produce stems long enough and strong enough for cutting. Emphasis is on individual flowers for close-up enjoyment in the yard, as fresh flowers for indoor decoration, competitive shows and general garden decoration. The flowers are nearly always double with twenty to fifty and more petals. They come in all shades except a true blue. Most are fragrant, some with a rich perfume that can fill a room.

It is becoming increasingly desirable to separate hybrid teas into exhibition kinds and decorative kinds. *The exhibition hybrid tea* is the mental image most of us conjure up when we hear or see the word "rose." It is the classic, long, pointed bud nearly always one to the stem, and these stems are especially fine for cutting. This group may not produce as many flowers in a season but each one is a dream. *Among the most popular:* 'First Prize', pink; 'Royal Highness', pink; 'Double Delight', red blend; 'Garden Party', white.

The decorative hybrid teas have flowers of quality virtually equal to the exhibition kinds and produce far more blooms and give a more colorful display. Stems are fine for cutting, but there may be occasional clusters of two or three flowers to a stem. Unless you are an exhibitor or a perfectionist, the decorative hybrid teas will be more satisfying. *Among the most popular:* 'Peace', yellow; 'Tropicana', orange; 'Mister Lincoln', red; Friend-

ship™ (variety: 'Linrick'), pink; 'Paradise', mauve; 'Double Delight', red blend (the all-purpose Hybrid Tea); 'Oregold', yellow; 'Honor', white.

GRANDIFLORAS: Vigorous plants of relatively tall growth and an abundance of flowers. They provide masses of color for garden decoration and have individual stems long enough for cutting. Here we have a combination of lots of color with well-formed buds and flowers of hybrid tea quality. In general, grandifloras are well suited for background plants and colorful displays while still providing stylish bloom on fine cutting stems. *Among the favorites:* 'Queen Elizabeth', pink; 'Sundowner', copper; 'Love', red and cream bicolor; 'Prominent', orange; 'Arizona', bronze; 'John S. Armstrong', red.

FLORIBUNDAS: Worldwide the most popular class of rose because of their profuse blooming and little need for care. They come in the full range of rose colors in a wide range of flower sizes. Ideally, floribundas should be planted in groups of three or more and are most effective massed fifty or more to a bed. They have a place in almost any landscape or garden planting for all-season color and added interest. Floribundas divide themselves into two groups.

DECORATIVE FLORIBUNDAS have masses of bloom in clusters which come in waves through the season. Flowers range from five petal singles to fully double mostly two to three inches across. The plants grow from 18" to 3 1/2', compact, lots of foliage, free flowering and especially hardy. *Among the favorites:* 'Charisma', multicolor; 'Europeana', red; 'Rose Parade', pink; 'Bahia', orange.

Large-flowered floribundas are fully as colorful as the decorative hybrid teas but also have large flowers, often one to the stem, fully double, of good form and all the newest colors. Plants are compact, floriferous and neatly formed. A develop-

10

ment of recent years, they add a new dimension and excitement to garden plantings. *Among the favorites*: 'Cherish', pink; 'Apricot Nectar', apricot; 'Saratoga', white; 'Angel Face', mauve.

MINIATURES: Originally these were diminutive forms of hybrid teas and floribundas with plants seldom exceeding twelve inches and blooms the size of a quarter. Today many approach floribundas in plant and flower size. They are compact, well-branched, with dense growth and leaves and flowers complementing the scale of the plant. Floriferous and often more hardy than their larger counterparts, miniature roses are becoming increasingly popular as garden, landscape and indoor plants. *Among the favorites*: 'Chipper', coral pink; 'Gold Coin', yellow; 'Starina', orange-red; 'Red Cascade', dark red; 'Cinderella', white; 'Bo-Peep', pink; 'Holy Toledo', copper.

PATIO ROSES: Coming into increasing use are these plants with relatively large, colorful flowers on a moderate size plant, vigorous and continuously flowering. Well suited for compact gardens and container growing for balconies, porches and patios.

TREE ROSES (*Standards*) are not a class of roses but a form of bush-rose bud grafted on a long-stemmed understock to form a trunk. Regular tree roses are hybrid teas, grandifloras or floribundas on trunks 30" to 36" high. Patio trees are small-flowered floribundas or patio roses on trunks 18" to 24" high. Miniature trees are miniature roses on trunks 10" to 15" high.

Tree roses make beautiful garden accents and give an added dimension to plantings. In colder areas they require special winter protection. (Tree roses are not shown on the accompanying classification diagram since they do not form a class of roses.)

POLYANTHAS AND HYBRID POLYANTHAS: This group falls between the old heritage roses and the modern floribundas. Very free flowering, in clusters, they were especially popular in the first third of this century. Low growing and especially hardy but with somewhat small flowers. The "Koster" types, 'Cecile Brunner' (Sweetheart rose) and 'China Doll' are still in commerce.

FLORA-TEA, MINI-FLORA AND DECORS: These are commercial trademarks developed to describe types of roses for merchandising purposes. They are descriptive and appropriate to the kinds of roses to which they are applied.

HERITAGE ROSES: Those that were grouped as "Old" roses, and which were developed in the nineteenth century fall in this class. For the most part they came directly from species roses and include Alba, Bourbon, Centifolia, Damask, Gallica, Moss, Noisette and Rugosa types. (More on these in the article titled "Old Garden Roses.")

Climbing Roses

CLIMBERS: Vigorous roses producing long, supple canes which lend themselves to training on supports such as fences, arbors, buildings and nearly any type of structure. Since roses do not entwine or have tendrils or any means of attaching themselves, they must be fastened to their support.

EVERBLOOMING CLIMBERS of today present a curtain of color in their spring bloom followed by additional bloom almost continuously through the season. Many are of hybrid tea quality and size, with good cutting stems.

SPRING-BLOOMING CLIMBERS: bloom only in spring and are often the hardiest type of rose. They make up in vigor what they lack in continuous bloom.

Climbing forms of bush roses are known as sports (mutations). They produce flowers of exactly the same type as the bush forms from which they come.

11

'Peace', a hybrid tea, is an all-time favorite.

Often these climbers are less hardy and are not recommended for colder areas of the United States.

Climbers are ideal as screens which can be impenetrable to man or animal and provide color through most of the growing season. They can be trained vertically, horizontally or up and over a pergola or archway. Climbers soften harsh architectural features and decorate fences most effectively. They are ideal to define areas, whether a small garden in the corner of a yard or the limits of an athletic field. *Among the most popular:* 'Blaze', red; 'Golden Showers', yellow; 'America', coral; 'Red Fountain', red; 'New Dawn', pink.

Shrub and Ground Cover Roses

SHRUB: A catch-all class of roses which do not clearly belong in any other group. They are less formal plants coming in a wide range of sizes and forms. They include both upright, free-standing bushes and those which are prostrate and trail along as ground covers.

FREE-STANDING SHRUBS: These grow broadly upright with canes that tend to arch outward forming a plant which is broader than it is high. Flowers come at the ends of the canes and on branches along the canes. *Spring-blooming shrubs* are those which flower only in spring. *Everblooming shrubs* grow vigorously, but not necessarily large, to flower almost continuously through the season.

Both types frequently set yellow, orange or red fruit which add color during the fall and winter. The fruit often

12

Jackson & Perkins breeder Keith Zary inspects a collection of miniature roses.

attracts birds and small game for the seed in the fruit. The fall and winter color of the fruit makes shrub roses especially attractive for yard, garden and commercial landscapes. Large kinds can be used for specimen or mass plantings and compact types for hedging, fences and bank covers. *Among the favorites*: Carefree Beauty™ (variety: 'Bucbi'), pink; 'Gartendirector Otto Linne', pink; 'Golden Wings', yellow.

GROUND COVERS: Usually vigorous roses which grow outward, almost prostrate or slightly mounded. They can be *spring-blooming* or *everblooming*. Interest is increasing as more everblooming kinds are introduced. *Among the favorites*: 'Sea Foam', white; 'New Dawn', pink; 'Max Graf', pink. 🍎

'Olympiad', a hybrid tea.

13

PLANTING ROSES

R. C. ALLEN

Whoever first gave the impression that roses are difficult to grow did the gardening community an injustice because there are few plants that will give as much pleasure for the effort expended. Because the rose is the embodiment of refinement and perfection among flowers, it is only natural that gardeners try hard to grow bushes and blooms that live up to the ideals pictured in catalogs or seen in rose shows. But even an imperfect rose will bring beauty and joy to the beholder.

Location and Soil Preparation

Unless the spot selected for planting roses has a minimum of six hours of full, or nearly full, sunlight a day, it will not be a desirable one. In general the more sunlight, the better growth and flowering. If one has a choice, it is better to have sun in the morning so that the opening blooms are not subjected to the bright sun during the hottest part of the day.

Soil drainage is another factor. Roses will not thrive in wet, soggy, poorly-drained soil, and it is futile to plant them in such a location. The best solution is to place the beds where drainage is naturally satisfactory. In severe situations

R.C. ALLEN *of Tucson, Arizona, is the former President of the American Rose Society and Director Emeritus of Kingwood Center in Mansfield, Ohio.*

drain tile should be installed, or raise the level of the beds eight or ten inches above ground level.

Nearness to large shrubs or trees should be avoided. Because of the fertilizing, watering, and other cultural practices, their roots may invade the rose beds and compete for nutrients and moisture. Fortunately roses are tolerant of invading roots if sufficient fertilizer and water are supplied. Planting closer than two feet from walls should also be avoided.

Air circulation is more important in the location of a large garden than where just a few beds are involved. Rarely do roses thrive in a sunken-type garden where the air does not move freely around the plants. In windy locations, too much air movement at certain times may make some type of windbreak protection desirable. Roses are more likely to do best where the air flows away from the beds rather than settling around them making the area subject to late spring or early fall frosts.

Any moderately fertile soil will grow good roses with little special preparation. Most garden soils, however, can be improved by incorporating fairly large quantities of peat moss, compost, leaf mold or well-rotted stable manure. Such organic materials should be spaded deeply and thoroughly into the soil. Working in superphosphate at the rate of three pounds/100 sq. ft. of ground area is also desirable in most localities. Preparing the soil well ahead of planting is advantageous.

Having the soil tested for alkalinity or acidity is a good precaution although roses are tolerant of a wide range of pH values. If the soil is very acid (pH 5 or lower) ground limestone should be mixed thoroughly into the soil at the rate of three to ten pounds/100 sq. ft. depending upon the degree of acidity. If the soil is distinctly alkaline (pH 7.5 or higher) an application of powdered sulphur at the rate of three pounds/100 sq. ft. will in time help reduce the alkalinity. The optimum pH value for roses is about 6.5.

Purchasing and Planting Time

Since more than a thousand different kinds of roses (varieties or cultivars) are offered by mail-order nurseries and garden centers, the choice is nearly unlimited if not bewildering. The American Rose Society offers a *Handbook for Selecting Roses* which gives the national rating of the cultivars available in the United States. The All-America Rose Selections recommendations are also good to follow. When you visit a rose show or a public garden, jot down the names of those roses that appeal to you. Most local rose organizations issue lists of the cultivars that do best in their localities.

Several different types of rose plants are available. First are the bare-root plants obtained by mail from nurseries that specialize in roses as well as those with general seed and plant catalogues. Many garden centers and large chain stores offer bare-root roses at planting time. Second are packaged plants, which are essentially bare-root except that the roots are wrapped in a moist medium and often the tops are covered with wax to retard drying out.

Third are the "preplanted" carton roses, a new type that has been gaining prominence in recent years. These are usually quality plants that have been planted in a good soil mixture in a biodegradable carton so that all the gardener needs to do is dig the hole in prepared soil and set in the carton according to the directions. Still another type is the canned or potted rose. These can be obtained anytime during the growing season from most garden or nursery centers. By and large, mail-order bare-root roses from rose specialists are considered best by most gardeners because they are invariably top grade stock according to the standards of the American Association of Nurserymen.

PREFERRED TIMES FOR PLANTING

Zone			
	1	Pacific Northwest	February, March
	2	Pacific Seaboard	January, February
	3	Southwest	Late December, January
	4	South Central	Late January, February
	5	Mid-South	February, March
	6	Subtropical	December, January
	7	North Central	April, Early May
	8	Eastern Seaboard	March, Early April
	9	Northeast	April, Early May

Prepare the planting site carefully.

Carton roses are planted in biodegradable bags.

Bare-root, packaged and preplanted bushes should be set out as soon as the soil can be worked in the winter or early spring, or in general while the plants are dormant and well before much vegetative growth begins. Most mail-order nurseries will ship at the proper time for planting. Since these dates vary greatly in different sections of the country the table on page 15 keyed to the regional map of the United States may be helpful. The suggested dates are only approximate and may vary within a single state because of differences in altitude and latitude. The principle is to plant as early as possible after the soil can be worked.

Water newly planted rose bushes.

Read the directions on carton roses and follow them carefully.

Planting and Post-planting Care

The steps in planting are simple, but one should pay attention to details because they often make the difference between a good start and a poor one. When mail-order plants arrive they should be planted immediately. If a delay of two or three days is necessary, the carton should be opened, the plants sprinkled lightly with water, then closed and stored in a cool place. Some gardeners like to place the plants in a tub of water for a few hours before planting, but under no circumstances should they be left in the water for more than eight hours. If for any reason it is necessary to hold the plants for more than a few days, it is best to remove the plants from the box and bury them in the ground to prevent drying out; this should be no longer than two weeks.

The first step in planting is to inspect each bush carefully and cut off any broken branches or roots. Most nurseries now ship with the tops cut back to the proper height for planting, but if the canes are excessively long they should be cut back to ten to twelve inches above the bud union, the knuckle-like swollen area where the top joins the rootstock.

Dig the hole large enough to accommodate the roots so that they can be spread out in a natural position. This means a hole fifteen to twenty-four inches in diameter and twelve to fifteen inches deep. The soil used to fill in around the roots should be mixed with about one-fourth peat moss or compost which helps to improve aeration, hold moisture and stimulate new root growth. It helps to make a cone-shaped mound of the mixture in the bottom of the hole, set the plant on it and then adjust the plant to the proper depth.

The depth at which the plant is set depends upon the climate. In localities where the temperature may drop to 0

BBG's rosarian, Stephen Scanniello, at work with volunteer Ruth Lutz.

degree F or lower, it is well to keep the bud union one or two inches below the general level of the soil. In less severe climates it does not need to be so deep and may be set at ground level, taking into account any settling that may occur.

Once the position is established, spread the roots in a natural position so that the main ones do not overlap. Then start working the peat moss or compost and soil mixture around the roots, preferably with the hands, so that no air spaces are left around the roots. When the hole is about two-thirds full, fill the rest of the space with water so that the soil is brought into close contact with the roots. When the water has drained away, fill in the rest of the soil, firm well and water again thoroughly.

In zones 1, 2, 3, and 6 (see page 15),

17

space hybrid teas and grandifloras 3 to 4 feet apart; zones 4, 5, and 8: 2 1/2 to 3 feet; zone 7: 2 to 2 1/2 feet, and in zone 9: 18 to 24 inches. Floribundas may be planted somewhat closer. Zones 1, 2, 3, and 6: 2 1/2 to 3 1/2 feet; zones 4, 5, and 8: 2 to 3 feet; zone 7: 2 to 2 1/2 feet; zone 9: 18 to 24 inches.

Roses should be protected as soon as they are planted to keep the canes from drying out before shoots begin to develop. The most common method is to mound soil around the plants, practically covering them. As soon as shoots start to grow the soil should be removed gradually.

Another method is to cover the plants with large shopping bags with the top corners cut down about four inches so that the edges can be folded back and covered with soil to hold the bags in place. After a couple of weeks the bags can be slit at the top and the plants inspected. If growth is starting the bags may be removed gradually.

Still another method is to cover the plants with Hot-tents. These are over-sized waxed paper hotcaps used by market gardeners that can be placed over the plants. When growth starts, they are opened at the top and eventually removed.

Watering newly-set bushes is necessary unless there is adequate rainfall to keep the ground moist. Moisture stress is reduced which is important in the development of strong vigorous shoots.

While the foregoing suggestions refer primarily to bare-root plants, the same recommendations apply to packaged roses. With these, however, it is desirable to soak the entire plant for several hours in water after removing the packing material.

The preplanted bushes in cartons (which should not be confused with packaged bare-root plants) are the easiest to handle. All that is necessary is to set the carton to the proper level and fill in around it with the peat moss-soil mixture and water thoroughly. Repeated watering is likely to be necessary until the roots have grown out of the decomposing carton.

Canned or potted roses require no special treatment except to make sure that the hole is at least six inches larger and deeper than the size of the container. Place some of the soil mixture in the bottom, remove the plant without disturbing the roots, fill in with soil, and water thoroughly. For about three weeks, watering must be repeated as if the plant were still growing in the container.

Miniature roses, which may be bare-root or potted, should be planted in well-prepared soil and set one to two feet apart.

General Suggestions

A few other suggestions may make future care easier and perhaps improve the quality of the growth. It is convenient if the beds contain but two rows of plants to facilitate the usual cultural practices.

Climbing roses will need support which should be installed before the roses are planted. Climbers are spaced at least six feet apart or even more if they are being grown on trellises or fences.

Tree roses budded on five or six foot understocks are attractive but except in the most favorable climates (zones 1-6) may require more specialized treatment than is easily provided. They may be planted bare-root, but to keep the tops from drying out they must be kept watered, the trunks wrapped with tree-wrap, and the tops covered with moist sphagnum moss in some type of bag, preferably a polyethylene type. Some firms shipping bare-root tree roses supply special bags and moss. Potted tree roses can also be obtained from some garden centers. ❦

P R U N I N G R O S E S

GEORGE HAIGHT

Roses are pruned for several reasons: to produce better flowers; to keep the plant shapely and within bounds; to encourage new basal growth and thus renew the plant. In general, the more severely a plant is pruned, the fewer flowers it will have, but they will be of larger size. Growers who exhibit their blooms at rose shows often follow this practice. A lighter pruning will produce a greater abundance of flowers, making this the more practical method for the average gardener who is interested in having a mass of color in his garden.

Timing and How to Start

Pruning is best done toward the end of the dormant season, just before the buds begin to swell. In mild climates, pruning may start in late December or January, but in cold parts of the East and Midwest it is best delayed until March or April. In either area it should be completed before the new leaves emerge or the canes will "bleed" sap. If necessary, however, it is better to prune late, despite "bleeding," than not at all. Unpruned plants are a good source for infestation by overwintering insects and disease spores. The earlier you prune, the sooner new

GEORGE HAIGHT *is the Proprietor of Stocking Rose Nursery in San Jose, California.*

growth will force out. In the event of late frosts, more pruning may be necessary on damaged new growth to prevent malformed blooms and blind wood.

If you are fairly confident of your technique, it is faster to start at the bottom of the plant and work to the top. If you are a bit uncertain as to which canes to remove, start at the top and work down. It will take longer to make decisions about which branches to shorten or remove, but it is a safer approach as you can change your mind many more times.

To begin pruning, remove all dead, diseased or twiggy growth. Growth less than the diameter of a pencil should be eliminated. Older canes that have produced nothing but weak growth should be removed to the bud union (the knob at the base of the plant from which all the canes force out). Then select the canes you wish to retain to form the framework of the plant. Four to eight or more canes may be left depending on the size and age of the plant. An older, vigorous plant can support more canes. The new canes can be distinguished from the older wood by a richer reddish-brown color, smoother wood and brownish thorns. Older canes will be duller in color, have creases and cracks in them, and thorns that as a rule are grayish.

The canes you select to keep may be

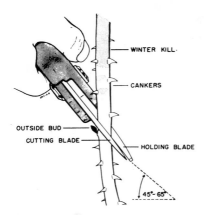

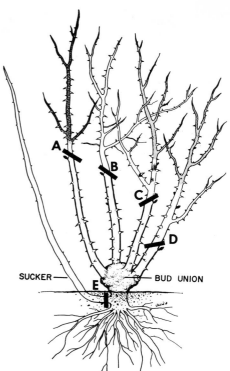

ABOVE, proper application of the hand pruner to the rose cane. The cutting blade must be on the lower side to insure a clean cut. RIGHT, principles of pruning a Floribunda. The cutting back of this class of rose is usually not as severe as on a Hybrid Tea.

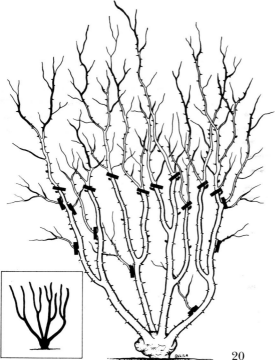

LEFT, principles of pruning Hybrid Tea roses:
A: high pruning for more and earlier blooms;
B: pruning to remove twiggy and cross branches;
C: pruning 1 inch below a canker;
D: severe pruning for removal of winter damage;
E: removal of sucker from understock.
"Bud union" marks region at which plant was grafted.

Prune with care using sharp tools.

all new ones if the plant has replenished itself generously during the past season. Generally, however, this is not the case, and you will probably select a combination of old and new canes. Choose carefully so you have a well-balanced, symmetrical plant. Some varieties do not renew themselves by sending out new basal shoots. In this event, retain the best of the older canes. The best flowers are produced on the newer wood, however, so some of the older canes may be removed to the bud union.

Cut close to the bud union and do not leave two-to-three-inch stumps that will be subject to rot and disease. Proceed to shorten the canes that grew during the past summer by one-third to one-half, but do not cut into the heavy old wood, as this may cause dieback. Always leave a lateral or branch on these old canes. Then thin out the smaller branches at the top and open up the centers of the plant for better air circulation, light penetration and greater ease in spraying. Remove cross branches.

Sometimes it is difficult to keep the symmetry of the bushes since the new canes may not have forced out in the most desirable location. Rather than cutting out good new or old canes because they are too close together, spread them apart by inserting a forked branch between them. This "spacer" may be left in place for the rest of the season.

As the plants begin to show leaves in the spring, some of the buds may grow strongly towards the center of the plant. These may be easily removed by pushing them off with your fingers. If there are

21

three buds forcing out from one node, it is well to push the two side or weaker buds off and let all the strength go into one cane. Candelabra canes which emerge from the bud union and grow so strongly that they tower above the rest of the plant may be controlled by pinching the tip when they are about fifteen inches tall. This will slow the growth and cause them to branch lower.

Suckers may appear on plants. These are long canes which have different foliage from the rest of the bush and sometimes smaller flowers of different color and form. A sucker grows from the rootstock and emerges from below the bud union. Suckers should be eliminated or they may outgrow your plant. They should be cut off at their point of origin. It may be necessary to use a trowel to dig below the ground level to see where they have started. Remove them completely, cutting into the root if you must.

Individual cuts should be made with sharp pruning shears to prevent mashing the canes. A small saw and long-handled lopping shears may be needed for heavier canes on older plants and getting into hard-to-reach places. Do not force your pruning shears when cutting heavy wood or you may throw them out of alignment. Cuts should be made at a 45-60 degrees angle about one-fourth inch above a bud. Where there is a leaf on the plant there is a bud. The new growth will grow in the direction the leaf is pointing, so the cut should be made just above a leaf that is pointing to the outside of the plant. Exceptions would be where the plant has grown too vigorously over a path or is spreading and you would like to confine it and get greater height. Then cut to an inside eye.

Treatment for Special Kinds

Hybrid teas and grandifloras may be cut back about one-third to one-half. Floribundas may be pruned more lightly—about one-fourth—with more branching left at the top. The older canes of climbing roses, such as the climbing hybrid teas of 'Peace', 'Chrysler' and 'Talisman', may be removed to the base. The newer canes which forced out during the past season but did not bloom will bloom the coming season. Do not shorten these canes to three feet as you will be cutting off wood that will bloom in the spring. It is well to leave a combination of old and new wood. The flowering spurs on the old wood may be cut back to two or three eyes. Leave six to eight canes to be tied horizontally on your fence as more flowers are produced if the canes are parallel to the ground rather than standing upright.

The old-fashioned and species roses are pruned lightly. Remove any dead wood and small spindly branches. The Bourbons and hybrid perpetuals may be pruned more severely. The teas may be cut back as you would a floribunda. Species such as 'Austrian Copper' may be thinned and shortened lightly. There will be a greater display of bloom if the canes can be arched and pegged to the ground.

Tree roses do not renew themselves with new basal canes for as long as regular bushes do, so remove few canes to the bud union. Keep the centers open and shorten the canes by about half.

After you have completed pruning, remove all leaves from the plant and rake the ground to eliminate a possible source of over-wintering insects or disease spores. It is well to give the plants a dormant spray, especially if you had problems with insects, mites or disease during the past growing season.

Roses are very rugged plants and will survive your pruning mistakes. A moderate and reasoned approach will produce an abundance of bloom for you in the coming season. ❧

WINTER PROTECTION

JOHN E. VOIGHT

rowing roses has long been the subject of rules as sententious as the Ten Commandments. The important matter of wintering these plants in cold parts of the country has itself been contradictory. Again and again, common sense comes to the rescue!

In areas where subzero temperatures are common, most types of modern roses need the heaviest winter protection or they will be weakened or lost completely. In areas where temperatures occasionally drop to zero or below, some protection may be needed, depending mainly on the exposure of the plants . (*Ed.* – None is necessary at Brooklyn Botanic Garden except for tree roses.) In the lower South or parts of the West where temperatures seldom get below 10 degrees F, it is unnecessary to protect roses.

The first principle of winter protection, regardless of the area, is to make sure the rose is in peak health as it goes into winter. A healthy rose bush is a hardy plant; it is as simple as that. A rose that has been beset with fungal and insect infestations, or one that has suffered drought, will not have the healthy leaf system required to manufacture sugar and starch for storage over winter. Watering practices in the colder climates,

JOHN E. VOIGHT *of Wauwatosa, Wisconsin, is Director Emeritus of Boerner Botanical Gardens (Milwaukee County Parks System).*

however, should generally cease in mid-September.

Other factors that should be considered are the ripeness of the wood, the length of the hardening-off period, autumn temperatures, rainfall, planting exposure and also the inherent nature of the varieties. Roses that are not protected when the temperature regularly drops below 20 degrees F for long periods of time may be damaged or killed regardless of area. The time to start protection will vary depending upon the season and locality. Here in Wisconsin it begins about October 20.

Methods for Cold Climates

SOIL MOUND. Nature provides the best material there is—soil. Good, old dirt soil. This popular method in the colder climates for protecting hybrid teas, grandifloras and polyanthas begins with tying

each bush with binder twine to make the plant compact. A quarter-inch mesh hardware cloth cylinder is placed around each individual plant. The cylinder is then filled with soil. Ground level should be checked in due time for settling and soil added if necessary.

The main purpose of the wire cylinder is to conserve soil. If only a few plants are involved, it is sufficient to merely mound the soil around the base of each plant. Miniature roses can be handled successfully in the same manner.

As soon as the ground is frozen solid, a layer of marsh hay is spread over the bed. Marsh hay is recommended because it is relatively weed-free and does not hold much moisture. Pruning of roses, regard-

less of climatic zones, should be left for the plant's dormancy period, ending as the new spring buds begin to swell. Bean hampers, if available, may be used and placed over soil-mounded plants to aid in salvaging more wood. Prune canes only to meet the height and diameter needs to clear contact with the basket.

In the colder regions many rose growers have had great success with styrofoam cones, which are handled the same as the bean hampers. It is advisable to purchase cones with a removable or hinged cover that can be opened for ventilation during warm days to prevent moisture from condensing inside. Cones and hampers should be anchored with soil or stones on the bottom flanges or they are apt to be blown over by high winds.

CLIMBERS AND TREE ROSES. In the colder climates, winter protection of climbers and tree roses becomes a unique problem. The common technique is to decide the direction in which the climber or tree rose is to rest. The plant is loosened from the soil in a semi-circle a foot or more from the base. Then the plant is bent down gently but firmly and pegged securely with wood lath. Boards may be placed around the climbers or tree roses to add insulation and conserve soil. Then the plant is completely covered with soil. Marsh hay, cornstalks or evergreen boughs are placed over the surface after the soil is frozen solid. This is a drastic and laborious method, yet it's the simplest and easiest way to bring climbers and tree roses through winter in cold climates.

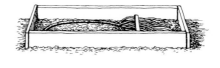

ILLUSTRATIONS BY EVA MELADY

24

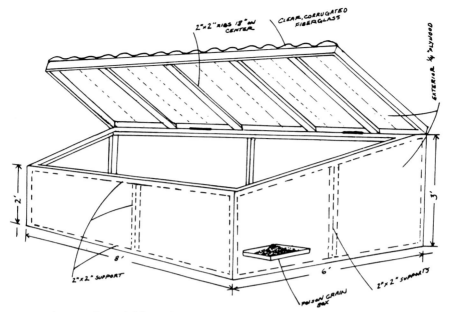

A plywood and fiberglass rose shelter, hinged for ventilation.

ILLUSTRATION BY JOHN E. VOIGHT

ROSE SHELTER METHOD. Another successful method for protecting roses in very cold climates employs a shelter over the entire bed. This is really nothing more than a portable coldframe. A well-ventilated structure with a light-transmitting roof gives excellent results. The roof is constructed of a clear, corrugated fiberglass that provides the necessary light and ventilation. The sides are constructed of a marine type of plywood, construction grade. To join the various sections, a door hinge with a removable pin works well. The roof should be constructed so it can be opened when the temperature gets warm. When there is danger of the temperature dropping to the mid-twenties, the top should be secured. Mice can be a problem so the shelter should be equipped with waterproof poison bait. In spring this shelter can double as a coldframe for hardening off plants that were housed indoors during the winter months.

OLDER CLASSES OF ROSES. Hybrid perpetuals don't need as much protection in subzero areas as hybrid teas. The best insurance may be to heel such roses with soil. The old-fashioned roses such as gallicas, moss, centifolias, damasks and other shrub roses are considered fully hardy without protection, even in southern Canada.

Removal of Winter Protection

The removal of winter protection requires timely judgment in severe climates. Marsh hay or similar covering material is gradually taken off, keeping the soil mounds intact until the danger of hard freezes has past. The soil mounds are then removed, preferably on an overcast day to avoid damage of new, tender growth. 🌿

GROWING ROSES IN CONTAINERS

ELVIN MCDONALD

If, as it is alleged, Cleopatra grew roses in containers on her barge, then the idea of the movable rose is hardly new. However, it is a practice that did not become widespread in North America until well after World War II, an offspring you might say of the marriage of two increasingly popular activities: terrace and patio living and container gardening. For the person whose outdoor gardening space is limited, perhaps, to a high-rise terrace, hardly any other plant can offer what the rose does—flowers throughout the growing season, fragrance, bouquets to enjoy fresh indoors, then sweet-smelling petals to add to potpourri.

Another reason so many of us are growing roses in containers is the vast improvement since the early 1960's of the miniatures. There are now miniatures in virtually every color found in other roses, plus varieties with mossing like the old-fashioned moss roses, miniature standards or trees two to three feet tall and hanging-basket types.

The other major reason people are growing roses in pots is because local nurseries and garden centers now sell rosebushes of all types—hybrid tea, grandiflora and floribunda—already growing in containers. This means that by the time roses are blooming in outdoor gardens in your area you can go to a nursery and select the varieties you like best by seeing and smelling real blooms instead of looking at catalog photographs. On the other hand, if you want some adventure, it can be just as much fun and fully as rewarding to select from catalogs, or to purchase containerized roses locally which may show buds but have no open flowers for you to sniff and admire.

For Best Performance

The single most important thing to remember if you want to be a rosarian whose roses have mobility is that they need soil that is constantly moist. If the soil dries out severely even one time the bush will suffer tremendous stress which you will see by the number of dead leaves and withered new growth tips.

Since roses need at least a half day of direct sun, this means that there will be considerable heat buildup in and around the containers, especially if they are placed on an exposed terrace or rooftop. Standard-size rosebushes need containers at least twelve inches in diameter and as deep or deeper. The miniatures will do well in six-inch pots. Obviously, the larger the container, the better it will

ELVIN MCDONALD *is Director of Special Projects at the Brooklyn Botanic Garden.*

retain moisture. For this reason, you will probably have better luck with the miniatures if you group several together in one sizable planter, perhaps eight inches deep and two feet in diameter; a container of this size will hold five bushes with perhaps one miniature tree in the center. Remember that the soil in unglazed clay will dry out more quickly than that in other types of containers.

Container roses need a rich, well-drained potting soil. You can mix your own by combining two parts each of packaged all-purpose potting soil and sphagnum peat moss with one part each of clean, sharp sand (or perlite) and well-rotted or dehydrated cow manure. Before adding this mix to the container, place a layer of drainage material in the bottom; this can be an inch of pebbles or pot shards in a small pot or shallow planter for miniatures, and up to two inches in deep pots, tubs or planters twelve inches in diameter or larger.

To plant, remove the rose from the container in which it has been growing. Place the rootball in its intended container with enough potting soil underneath so that it will be at the same level in the soil as before. Pack potting soil all around so there will be no air pockets, then saturate with water. Begin feeding regularly with a rose fertilizer two weeks later and continue throughout the growing season. To control insect pests and diseases, apply an all-purpose systematic rose pesticide in granular form to the soil surface, then water well.

Winter Care North and South

In climates where winter temperatures regularly drop below 20 degrees F, containerized roses will have a higher rate of survival if moved, after the first killing frost, to an unheated garage or out-building, a deep coldframe or pit greenhouse.

Prune back any excessively long or tall canes at this time, but wait until planting-out weather in the spring to do the full-fledged annual pruning. Be sure the growing medium is nicely moist at the time of winter freeze-up. If you must keep container roses on a high-rise terrace or rooftop in a cold climate, push them all together against a protecting wall, moisten the soil thoroughly, mulch generously with salt hay, then cover with a tarpaulin tied securely in place.

If you live in a mild climate where winter temperatures rarely drop below 20 degrees F, containerized roses can be brought through the dormant season any convenient place outdoors, perhaps left standing exactly where they have been growing. Just be sure the growing medium is moist at all times, especially during any period of sunny, unseasonably warm weather. Also, if the wintering-over place is exposed to strong winds, as on a high-rise terrace, prune back any canes subject to whipping, otherwise roots may be broken.

Other tips for success with roses in containers include:

At the beginning of the growing season in the second and succeeding years, use your fingers to remove the top two or three inches of old growing medium and replace with fresh; this is called top-dressing and takes the place of all-out repotting.

If you live where summers tend to be extremely hot and dry, devise some means for keeping the containers shaded while the rosebushes themselves are in the sun. This keeps soil temperatures down and reduces the amount of watering you'll have to do.

Wood cleats placed under wooden planter boxes, large clay pots or other containers will increase air circulation, thus reducing heat buildup, while at the same time assuring rapid runoff of excess moisture. 🌾

A ROSE GARDEN WITHOUT PESTICIDES

TIM RHAY

A community asset for decades, the George E. Owen Municipal Rose Garden has always rewarded visitors with its beautiful formal plantings in the classic European/English style, but it is worth a visit today for additional reasons. For the last three years, by applying the principles of integrated pest management, the staff of the Owen Garden has been able to maintain demanding aesthetic standards with no need for insecticide or fungicide sprays.

Eugene, Oregon's Parks Services Division formally adopted IPM for all vegetation and pest control operations in 1980. IPM stresses the use of naturally occurring controls and cultural practices; pesticides are applied only when infestation levels reach a "threshold." In agriculture, where IPM was first applied, this threshold is determined by economic criteria. By substituting realistic

maintenance standards for the economic criteria and setting treatment thresholds below the point where those standards would be compromised, Eugene has adapted the IPM strategy to the full range of grounds maintenance weed and pest control situations.

The program has been an unqualified success, enabling the division to dramatically reduce pesticide use without negative impacts on maintenance standards or costs. The rose garden's program has been particularly satisfying because, in the beginning, it was generally accepted that dramatic reductions in pesticide use would not be possible there.

Even the gardeners were surprised by their success. "Ten years go, I would have said we couldn't stop spraying," says Paul Heard, assistant to Head Gardener Glenn Thompson. But both men see significant advantages to their IPM approach and, surrounded by beauty that speaks louder than words of the

TIM RHAY *is Turf and Grounds Supervisor for the Eugene Parks Services Division in Eugene, Oregon.*

effectiveness of their methods, neither harbors a desire to return to the old days of pesticide-intensive rose care.

"It's a great relief," says Thompson. "It saves lots of money and time for other things." The savings are invested in a good cultural program that involves irrigation, fertilization, pruning, and transplanting. The idea is to keep the roses healthy, eliminating the need for spray programs.

Predatory insects help hold aphid populations below the level that would require insecticide application. Soap solutions have proven effective when the "treatment threshold" is reached, but their use is confined to identified infested plants rather than garden-wide treatments. This keeps non-target impact to a minimum (another principle of IPM) and helps to maintain the predator population. An updated irrigation system, installed in 1986, also has assisted. The modern irrigation heads do an effective job of "water blasting" aphids off of the foliage.

Disease control is similar but even more remarkable, because the need for pre-emptive fungicide applications at regular intervals is so widely accepted as necessary among rosarians. Indeed, even many who disapprove of chemical pesti-

BAKING SODA VERSUS BLACKSPOT

After three seasons of ongoing research, Cornell University plant pathologist R. Kenneth Horst has concluded that baking soda in water, with a touch of gardener's insecticidal soap, can help prevent or control the dreaded black spot, a fungal infection in roses.

In 1987, 1988 and 1989 'Pascali' and 'Mr. Lincoln' plants, chosen because of their susceptibility to fungal diseases, were sprayed every three or four days from mid-April through October with various concentrations of baking soda in water. The soap was added for more even coverage of the leaves and to help the solutions stick during the rain.

A 0.5 percent solution of baking soda was found to be most effective at preventing the disease. High concentrations of baking soda caused burning of leaves. Some cultivars were more sensitive than others to burning, and greenhouse plants appeared to burn easier than outdoor plants. Horst is continuing his research, and still isn't sure why the baking soda helps prevent black spot.

The most effective spray tested can be made up by adding five tablespoons of baking soda to five gallons of water. To this add a few drops of insecticidal soap recommended for the garden. Cornell suggests that you test your spray on both the old and new leaves of just a few roses. Try an application every other day for a week and note any brown discoloration or burning of the leaves. Don't spray your whole collection before testing for burning first!

29

cides will admit this and suggest that alternative plant materials be used, or at least only the most disease-resistant rose varieties — neither of which is a workable option in a garden such as Owen, with over 400 varieties on display. Thompson's and Heard's work has proven that it is possible to have it both ways — a beautiful, classic display garden on the one hand and little or no use of synthetic fungicides on the other.

Here, again, the foundation of the program is healthy plants, assisted by the natural micro-climate of the site and intelligent management. "It all starts with a thorough pruning in January," explains Heard. Weak, small growth that will not support a bloom is removed. Such growth is often where disease begins. Both men agree that healthy growth is rarely infested initally, unless it is near the weaker stems. Pruning techniques are assisted by good airflow throughout the site from a steady breeze off the adjacent Willamette River, a monthly fertilizer program throughout the growing season, adequate irrigation (timed for the early morning hours) and the thorough washing provided by the pop-up, shrub spray irrigation heads.

Thompson also believes his transplanting techniques contribute to the health and disease-resistance of the garden's roses. "Digging up roses and replanting them stimulates them," he says. The Garden staff moves and divides plants regularly. Early fall is considered the optimum time, but transplanting continues throughout the dormant season in a typical year. Roses are planted with the crown about two inches below the surface, causing the plant to root out on the crown. This avoids basal shoots from the grafted rootstock, and both the head gardener and his assistant believe it also contributes to winter-hardiness and disease-resistance.

Some rose varieties particularly prone to rust were moved from the upwind to the downwind side of the garden to inhibit the spread of this disease.

Another technique worth consideration is the grouping of disease-prone varieties together in blocks so that fungicide application can be limited when/if treatment of these plants becomes necessary. "There have always been varieties that didn't need spraying — they aren't susceptible," Thompson observes, adding that it is a waste of time to spray such plants. Biodegradable soap/sulfur fungicides for roses are also available on the market and can be tried before resorting to more toxic materials.

When Eugene's IPM program began, it was believed that a strong preventive program stressing dormant season applications of milder materials such as lime-sulfur and dormant oil would yield the lowest non-target impact without compromising necessary standards for disease control. This initial effort was successful in reducing necessary "growing season" treatments, but Thompson and Heard were convinced they could do even better. In 1985-6, they decided to try to do without any pre-emptive fungicide application.

At the Owen Municipal Rose Garden, Glenn Thompson's 24 years of site-specific rose care experience and Paul Heard's 11 years as his assistant have combined to produce a truly revolutionary system of insect and disease control without pesticides. Their success has surpassed all expectations, eliminating the regular use of synthetic insecticides and fungicides and earning in 1987, even while this was being done, a Certificate of Award as an "Outstanding Rose Garden" from All-America Rose Selections.

"I've visited gardens with intensive spray programs that had as much rust as Owen does without one," asserts Thompson. He also believes dried spray materials on foliage can be unsightly and that too-frequent use of pesticides has negative effects on the health and vigor of roses. As two examples, he cites damaged buds and shoots resulting from accumulations of dormant spray materials at the leaf axil and the plugging of stomata by miticide and fungicide applied to the underside of leaves. "We have enough to do around here without insulting the roses with spray," he says.

"I used to apply more pesticide than all the other applicators (in the Parks Division) combined," adds Heard. "Sometimes it's amazing what you can do without." ❧

THIS IS AN EDITED VERSION OF AN ARTICLE WHICH FIRST APPEARED IN THE JANUARY 1990 ISSUE OF **THE AMERICAN ROSE MAGAZINE.**

INDICATOR ROSES

Did you know that your rose garden has a built-in early warning system against diseases and pests? Assuming that you haven't installed some kind of sophisticated radar to detect low-flying cucumber beetles, your warning system probably consists of several indicator roses. Indicator roses are those plants which, because of their cultivar characteristics or their particular microclimate, are particularly susceptible to one or more diseases or pests.

These roses are usually the first to be attacked by unwanted garden visitors. By paying close attention to them, you can determine if and when an invasion has taken place. They will also give you an indication of the effectiveness of your pest control, watering, and other rose care procedures.

In our garden, we have identified several indicator roses for various problems:

BLACK SPOT: 'Jules Margottin' and 'Pink Parfait'. These two will start showing spots first.

POWDERY MILDEW: We fight this problem constantly and you might say all our roses are indicators for mildew. However, 'Garden Party' and 'Rosy Gem' are the ones we watch closest.

ANTHRACNOSE: 'Showbiz'. (This is probably a microclimate difference since the 'Europeana' we used to have in the same spot also got it routinely.)

SPIDER MITES: 'Folklore' and 'Honor'.

CUCUMBER BEETLES: Nearly all the white roses but 'Pascali' and 'Honor' seem to be attacked first.

LEAF BURN: 'Madras' is the most sensitive to heavy applications of spray materials in hot weather.

The indicator roses in your garden are probably different from ours. Learn which ones they are and use them to your advantage.

— Dr. Tom Hickey

REPRINTED WITH PERMISSION FROM THE ROSEBUD, THE BULLETIN OF THE EVANSVILLE ROSE SOCIETY IN INDIANA. DR. HICKEY IS THE EDITOR.

THREE COMMON ROSE DISEASES

POWDERY MILDEW

Powdery mildew is probably the most widely distributed and serious rose disease.

At 68 degrees F (20 degrees C) and near 100 percent humidity, conidia, or clusters of spores, begin to germinate two to four hours after they're deposited on a leaf. The first symptoms of the disease are slightly raised, blisterlike, often red areas on the upper leaf surfaces. The characteristic white growth of the fungus appears as discrete patches on the leaf surfaces of young leaves, which become twisted and distorted and commonly are completely covered with the powdery white growth. Older leaves may not be distorted, but circular or irregular areas may be covered with growth of the mildew fungus. Mature leaves usually aren't infected.

Fungal growth may develop first on succulent young stem tissues, especially at the base of thorns, and the growth persists when stems mature. New spring shoots that develop from dormant buds may become infected by the fungus overwintering in rudimentary leaves or bud scales. The fungus may also attack the flowers, especially unopened buds, resulting in flowers of poor quality.

Favorable Conditions

Temperature, relative humidity and the presence of free water play an important role in the development of powdery mildew disease. The optimal temperature at high humidity is 70 degrees F (21 degrees C) for germination of the conidia (spore clusters), and 64-77 degrees F (18-25 degrees C) for growth of the mycelia, or cobwebby filaments. The optimal humidity for germination of the spores is 97-99 percent. On the other hand, powdery mildew is inhibited by the presence of films of water on the leaf surfaces. During the late 1930s and early '40s, in fact, when spider mites on roses were controlled by frequent water sprays, powdery mildew was rarely a problem, although black spot was a serious one.

Control

Powdery mildew has been controlled mainly through the use of fungicidal sprays. Planting rose cultivars that are less susceptible can help. Ramblers, climbers and hybrid teas are generally very susceptible; wichuraianas are more resistant. Many new rose cultivars show resistance to powdery mildew. However, the resistance rarely lasts, because new strains of the powdery mildew fungus evolve.

Pruning infected shoots at the end of the season and destroying them in regions where winters are severe will help prevent the fungus from overwintering. Raking and destroying fallen leaves from around the bushes at the end of the season can also inhibit overwintering.

Plant diseases

O Ma Babbino
Puccini

BLACK SPOT

Black spot is another important disease that afflicts roses around the world.

Characteristic black spots develop on upper leaf surfaces. Leaf tissue surrounding the spots turns yellow, and this chlorosis expands throughout the leaf until it drops. In resistant cultivars or under unfavorable environmental conditions, only tiny black flecks may form and leaves may not turn yellow or fall.

Raised purple-red, irregular blotches develop on the immature wood of first-year canes of susceptible cultivars. The spots later become blackened and blistered; the lesions are often small and rarely kill branches but are extremely important in the survival of the pathogen over the winter.

Favorable Conditions

Leaves are most susceptible while they're still growing. Regardless of the relative humidity, the spores must be immersed in water and be continuously wet for at least seven hours for any infection to occur. A spore germinates in 9-18 hours on a moist leaf at 72-79 degrees F (22-26 degrees C).

The disease spreads when the spores are carried by rain or splashing water, by people during cultivation, or by insects. The fungus does not survive in the soil, and spores adhering to tools, benches, and so on remain viable no longer than a month. In areas with mild climates, the fungus remains active on the plant throughout the year. In cold areas, the fungus overwinters in fallen leaves or in infected canes.

Control

Good air circulation around bushes hastens drying and reduces black spot. Leaves should not be allowed to remain wet or at very high humidity for more than 7-12 hours. Excessive watering should be avoided during dark, humid weather.

Removing leaves from the ground and pruning canes that contain lesions will reduce overwintering of the pathogen.

Resistance to black spot in roses is rare. Cultivars that reportedly are highly resistant are 'David Thompson', 'Bebe Lune', 'Coronado', 'Ernest H. Morse', 'Fortyniner', 'Grand Opera', 'Lucy Cromphorn', 'Sphinx', 'Tiara', 'Carefree Beauty' and 'Simplicity'. In general, teas, hybrid teas, hybrid perpetuals, Pernetianas, Austrian briers and polyanthas are quite susceptible and rugosa hybrids, moss roses and wichuraianas are more resistant.

Researchers at Cornell University have had success preventing black spot with a solution of baking soda in water (see page 29).

RUST

Nine species of the rust fungus are found on roses. Although rust is generally widespread, it is more common in the western United States and other areas where cool temperatures and high moisture at certain times of the year are conducive to disease development.

The disease first appears on leaves and other green parts of the plant as powdery orange pustules, or blisters, usually on the lower leaf surfaces. In early spring, spore masses are not very conspicuous. As the pustules develop, they become visible on upper leaf surfaces as orange or brown spots. Young stems and sepals also may become infected.

Favorable Conditions

Spores from rust pustules are carried in the air and infect rose leaves through leaf openings. The optimal temperatures for disease development are 64-70

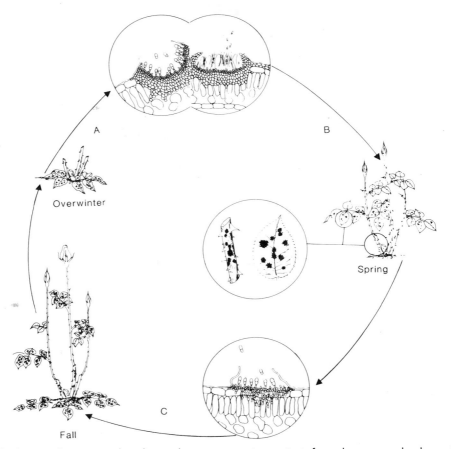

Black spot disease cycle. The pathogen overwinters in infected canes or buds and in fallen leaves (A). New shoots are infected from overwintering mycelium or from water-splashed conidia or airborne ascospores produced on fallen leaves, sometimes in the same lesion (B). Leaves and canes are infected during summer by airborne ascospores or water-splashed conidia produced on infected leaves (C).

degrees F (18-21 degrees C), and continuous moisture for two to four hours is essential for the disease to become established.

In late summer and early autumn, black pustules appear. The blisters can overwinter in the leaf and stem tissues and cause infections in spring.

Control

Removing infected leaves during the season and all old leaves left in winter helps prevent rust. Spring pruning of old canes will help prevent rust carry-over on canes.

Some cultivars are much more susceptible than others. Leaves of some cultivars may become covered with pustules and yet remain attached to the plant, while a single rust pustule on a leaflet of another cultivar will cause it to fall. Susceptible and moderately susceptible cultivars are

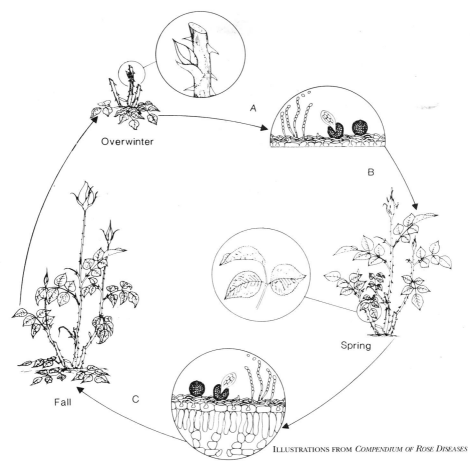

Overwinter

A

B

Spring

Fall

C

Powdery mildew disease cycle. The pathogen overwinters in infected canes or buds and in fallen leaves (A). New shoots are infected from overwintering mycelium or from conidia or ascospores produced on fallen leaves (B). Leaves and flowers are infected during the summer by airborne conidia or ascospores produced on infected portions of plants (C).

'Arlene Francis', 'Aztec', 'Baby Blaze', 'Betsy McCall', 'Blue Moon', 'Buccaneer', 'Christopher Stone', 'Chrysler Imperial', 'Circus', 'Confidence', 'Dearest', 'Elizabeth of Glamis', 'Embers', 'Fragrant Cloud', 'Fusilier', 'Golden Girl', 'Golden Masterpiece', 'Heat Wave', 'Helen Traubel', 'Jeanie', 'Josephine Bruce', 'Kordes Perfecta', 'Montezuma', 'New Yorker', 'Nocturne', 'Peace', 'Piccadilly', 'Pink Peace', 'Pink Radiance', 'Queen Eliza-beth', 'Siren', 'Spartan', 'Sutter's Gold', 'Talisman', 'The Doctor', 'Virgo', 'Vogue', 'Wendy Cussons', 'White Bouquet', 'White Knight' and 'White Swan'. Many new cultivars not on this list are also susceptible. ♥

ADAPTED FROM *COMPENDIUM OF ROSE DISEASES*, AUTHORED BY R. KENNETH HORST AND AVAILABLE FROM APS PRESS, 3340 PILOT KNOB ROAD, ST. PAUL, MN 55121.

BBG's Cranford Rose Garden.

ROSES IN THE LANDSCAPE

Ernest Wertheim

No palace revolution could ever tumble the rose from her status as Queen of the Flowers. Roses are the source of wines, dyes, medicaments, oils, perfumes, pomanders and potpourris. When they are in season, they are the most spectacular and conspicuous ornaments in the garden. Roses have decorated the grandest of feasts, have often been the flower of weddings, and are the symbol of love. No wonder then that many home gardeners wish to include the rose as a part of the landscape.

Planning

To decide where we might plant one rose, or several roses, or establish a rose garden, we should first concern ourselves with some of the basics of landscape

Ernest Wertheim *is a landscape architect with Wertheim, van der Ploeg & Klemeyer in San Francisco, California.*

design. The garden should provide a beautiful setting for the house and lovely vistas when seen from the windows. Garden spaces influence indoor comfort, and in the milder portion of the year can be developed into extensions of the living space of the house.

Home planning, then, must include both indoors and outdoors. It is a project for complete control of the space we live in, the things we see, and the use and maintenance of that space. What better place to relax than to be in the garden and absorb the beauty of the flowers of a rose garden, or inhale their wonderful perfume, or, if it is winter, to study the shape of the plants and prune away those old stocks so that new ones can take their place.

The challenges of home planning are similar throughout the country because human needs and desires are basically similar; it is the surrounding conditions which vary. All homes must provide in one way or another four main functions: public access, general living, work space, and private living.

The first thing to be done is to prepare a site plan illustrating the existing conditions. Two of the major requirements for the design of the garden are utility and beauty; spaces should be produced that are both useful and beautiful. Useful should mean comfortable, convenient, workable or productive, and beautiful means that the garden gives us a pleasant, inspiring or relaxing sensation. The garden may be warm or cool, calm or exciting, simple or intricate, formal or informal, colorful or quiet, and filled with vegetation or structures. If the garden is beautiful, we have an experience that is remembered, and we will wish to return.

'Altissimo', a climber, trained along a fence.

elevation

A garden must be developed so that there is a good relationship between house and garden, and between garden and neighbors. When it comes down to details each space within the garden must have a good relationship to another.

After a list of requirements for the outdoor areas has been prepared a "bubble" diagram can be completed; each "bubble" should be representative of the size required for a specific function, and its position in relationship to the other "bubbles" considered. The requirements may include such items as: driveway with space for guest parking; public access and private access to both the house and garden; service entrance, service yard, laundry yard and dog run; play area for children; swimming pool, ornamental pool or fountain; outdoor sitting area; low maintenance type garden; lawn area for visual effect and play; shade structure for both people and shade loving plants; arbor for vines or grapes; gardener's nook – greenhouse, lath house, potting bench, soil storage and tool storage; types of plant areas – perennial border, vegetable garden, flower garden, rose garden (formal or informal), space to grow fruit trees and berries.

When preparing this diagram, consideration should be given to sun and shade, warm and cold areas, direction of prevailing winds (both summer and winter), and private and non-private areas.

This "bubble" planning stage may take a little time or a lot, depending on how difficult the site might be, how exacting and complicated the requirements might be, and how well you are capable of visualizing the plan on paper. If you have trouble visualizing things on paper, you might get stakes and string and lay your diagram out on the site. Use a watering hose to create curved lines. It may be helpful to make a scale model of the site and study the relationship of the various elements. This is particularly true when dealing with a site that varies in grade.

Once you have arrived at a rough schematic solution that appears to answer all your requirements, the final design can commence. This is the stage when decisions must be made about the kinds of materials to be used; what precise form and arrangement to give them; how much construction and how much shelter; how to enrich the garden with fine colors, textures and forms; how to make drainage work; how to provide irrigation, lighting and spaces for garden sculpture.

Each decision affects the other. If for example a formal rose garden is to be included, it will influence the concept of the total design. Materials, forms and arrangement all go together. More construction means less planting and therefore more initial outlay, but less continuous maintenance (and vice versa). Enclosures and shelter are the primary forming elements of garden spaces giving them order, character and quality.

During the last forty years many changes have taken place in landscape design; it has become more sensitive, more sophisticated, more variable, and less bound by precedent and convention. Formal and informal design, once carefully segregated, have integrated and produced the diversified new rich forms. It is recommended that the homeowner read books by some of the well-known landscape architects in this country such as Douglas Baylis, Thomas Church, Garrett Eckbo, Lawrence Halprin, Dan Kiley, Robert Royston, Hideo Sasaki and John Ormsbee Simonds. Although these books may at times be heavy reading, they are full of good information and have many fine illustrations.

A Few Sketches for Using Roses

To return specifically to roses in residen-

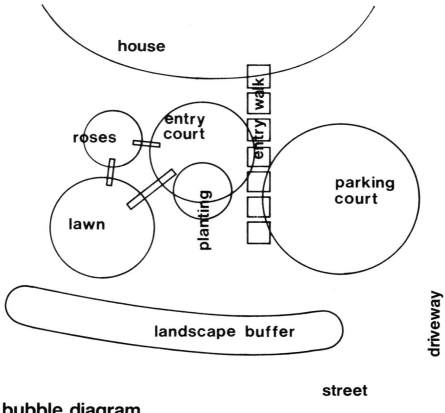

bubble diagram

ILLUSTRATIONS BY ERNEST WERTHEIM

Roses trained over arches, Butchart Gardens, Victoria, B.C., Canada.

tial gardens, several sketches have been prepared to illustrate their use. The varieties mentioned are those used on these plans. Individual tastes and climatic conditions may dictate selection of different varieties. Plan No. 1 is a partial design of a front garden in California. Along the street on the public side of the fence is a mass planting of rose 'Circus'. On the fence is the climbing rose 'Mrs. Sam McGredy'. The fence is of wrought iron with brick pillars, which gives the owner and passerby an opportunity to see the planting at both sides of it.

The hybrid tea roses are located to the side of the driveway with dwarf English box (*Buxus sempervirens* 'Suffruticosa') as an edging (not hardy everywhere). The varieties of hybrid teas are 'Tropicana', 'Fragrant Cloud', 'Summer Sunshine' and 'Peace'. Care should be taken to use the less vigorous varieties to the front of the bed with the taller ones to the rear. Because there are several bushes of one variety, the chance of picking a bouquet is increased.

Pyracantha was selected to give color through its orange or red berries in the fall and early winter when the roses are declining to bloom. For early spring bloom a crab apple, *Malus scheideckeri*, with attractive pale pink flowers, was placed on the north side of the rose planting so that it will not throw shade on the roses. This California garden has roses in bloom between late April and December.

Plan No. 2 illustrates a front garden which is partially private and partially exposed to the street. The visitor has to enter through a gate and is then surprised by the very intimate space where the owner can enjoy the sun without being seen from the street. The front patio is completely enclosed. On the outside of the enclosed patio is a small lawn which is edged by rose 'Sarabande'. It provides color in this California garden for more than six months. There is little maintenance connected with this planting. The edging between the lawn and the roses is a compact form of lavender, *Lavandula angustifolia* 'Hidcote'. The groundcover along the street is Sargent juniper (*Juniperus chinensis* 'Sargentii', and the trees are *Malus* 'Katherine', a pink, double-flowering crab apple. Inside the brick planter is a light pink flowering cherry (*Prunus yedoensis* 'Akebono') with annuals below. The flowering cherry blooms earlier than the crab apple; both of them, however, are through before the rose starts to flower. The lavender blooms during the summer. Winter color is provided by the red berries of a California native shrub, toyon (*Heteromeles arbutifolia*).

Plan No. 3 has roses as the dominant feature in a wall-enclosed garden. The vista created by the lawn leads the eye from the terrace to the fountain and the semi-circular brick wall. The flowering trees on the sides and end will bloom prior to the roses, and they give a feeling of height, and help to create a sense of enclosure.

The four hybrid tea roses in each square should be the same variety. Darker reds could be used near the fountain with the color in each square getting lighter as they come toward the terrace and entrance to the garden. All the beds are edged with a clipped hedge such as boxwood, hebe, lavender or germander. The wall that encloses the garden is brick.

Plan No. 4 is a small San Francisco garden which was designed to be viewed from a bay window. The fountain creates a lovely water effect and the pool is stocked with exotic fish. The garden lights provide the owner with a nice night effect.

The wood platform provides a small space for relaxing and sunning, and the brick walls create complete privacy. The garden gate leads to the street but is not the main entrance to the house. The large tree is an existing English holly (*Ilex aquifolium*) which is heavily covered with red berries during winter. Around the edge of this beautiful holly are 'Peace' roses, and along the brick walk is a mass planting of miniature roses. Early spring color is provided by the fragrant white flowers of *Rhododendron* 'Forsteranum'.

Climbers

Mention should be made of the spectacular climbing rose 'Mrs. Sam McGredy', which is on a split rail fence at the Sunset Magazine headquarters in Menlo Park, California. This planting extends over two hundred feet with each plant being located between two rail-type posts about eight feet on center. When in bloom this lovely, fragrant rose makes a beautiful display, and when not in bloom the young reddish foliage is lovely to look at, in particular with the green lawn as a backdrop. Maintenance is relatively easy because the

Wisteria and roses at Butchart Gardens.

gardener can get at the plants from two sides. This rose, not readily available any more, is listed by Stocking's Rose Nursery in San Jose, California.

When a climbing rose is used on a porch post, a variety should be chosen that is not too rampant in habit or growth; 'High Noon' or 'Royal Gold' would be good choices. The vigorous climbers should be used mainly on walls or arbors where they have plenty of room to expand. Pruning of the more vigorous roses may present a problem for the average homeowner.

Climbing roses can be successfully used on banks, not only for beauty but for erosion control. A favorite rose in mild climates for this purpose is the yellow-flowered form of the Banksia rose (*Rosa banksiae* 'Lutea'). This rose is not easy to find, although it is listed in the current catalog of Monrovia Nursery in

41

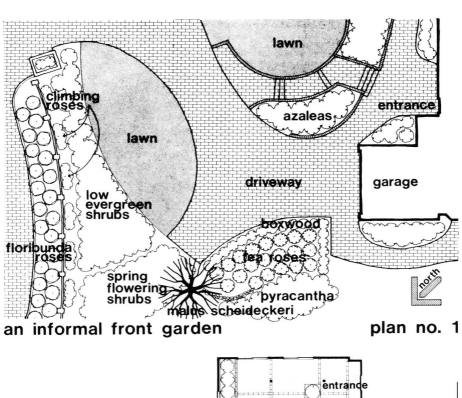

an informal front garden

Labels in plan no. 1:
lawn
climbing roses
lawn
azaleas
entrance
driveway
garage
low evergreen shrubs
boxwood
floribunda roses
tea roses
spring flowering shrubs
pyracantha
malus scheideckeri
north

plan no. 1

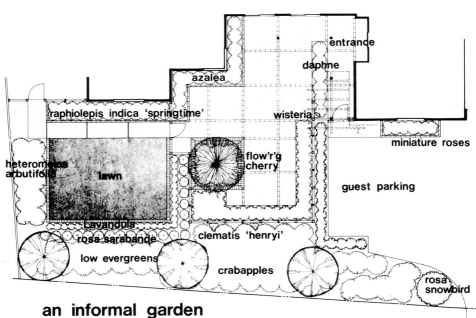

an informal garden

Labels in plan no. 2:
entrance
daphne
azalea
raphiolepis indica 'springtime'
wisteria
miniature roses
heteromeles arbutifolia
lawn
flow'r'g cherry
guest parking
lavandula
rosa sarabande
clematis 'henryi'
low evergreens
crabapples
rosa snowbird

plan no. 2

42

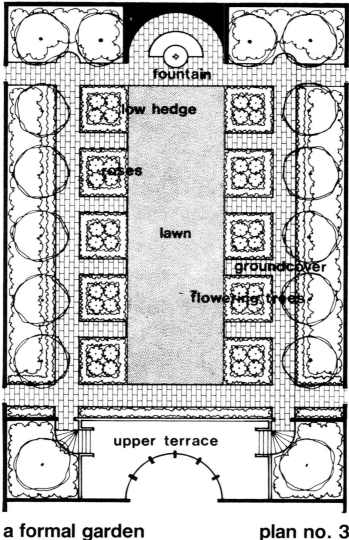

fountain

low hedge

roses

lawn

groundcover

flowering trees

upper terrace

a formal garden   plan no. 3

Azusa, California, a leading wholesaler. This author understands that Monrovia's plants are on their own roots which creates better plants for the purpose of bank planting. The yellow form also makes a lovely display when used on fences. The white form 'Alba Plena' is equally good. Both are thornless or nearly so.

In mild climates *Rosa bracteata* 'Mermaid' can be used on large banks where there is a lot of room for expansion. In cold climates the white-flowered *Rosa wichuraiana* would be a good choice for a ground cover. Both 'Mermaid' and *R. wichuraiana* need plenty of space.

'Snowbird' is another fine climber that

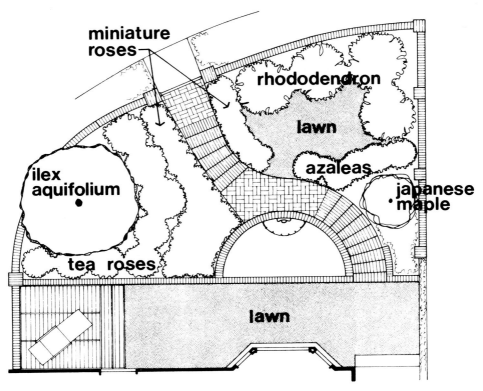

miniature roses

rhododendron

lawn

ilex aquifolium

azaleas

japanese maple

tea roses

lawn

small garden

can be used on banks. The soft green foliage is a lovely contrast to the abundant white flowers which are fragrant. This rose can be used as an accent between a mass planting of low junipers or weeping English yew (*Taxus baccata* 'Repandens').

Some Uses for Different Kinds

Roses are not only for the home garden but are useful on commercial and institutional landscapes as well. Ted Osmundson, landscape architect for Kaiser Industries Headquarters in Oakland, California, has successfully used masses of 'Sarabande' and other floribundas on the building's roof garden. The City of Walnut Creek, California, has also used 'Sarabande' to fine effect; it planted five

plan no. 4

hundred in a downtown media strip, and the roses are doing well and are not affected by auto exhaust fumes.

Most roses need attention and the gardener who devotes a lot of love and care is often rewarded with excellent results. There are, however, some roses that don't require much, if any, care. In a revegetation project in the high Sierras near Lake Tahoe, *Rosa woodsii ultra-montana* was used, and it was found that this plant not only tolerated drought conditions well, but produced more growth per year than some of the other native shrubs. This rose was used in mass, and although it is not spectacular when in bloom, the pink blossoms appear throughout summer, followed by colorful fruit in autumn. The plants survive without supplements or feeding, and with no water other than the natural rain and snow fall. This rose has underground runners which help make it valuable for erosion control.

Miniature roses should also be mentioned. They can be used individually or in groups. Some of the miniatures have been used very successfully in rock gardens, while others have been used as edging to flower beds, or in mass plantings around an ornamental pool. In mild climates the miniature rose is used in low pottery bowls and placed at entrance porches, on patios or on balconies of apartments. The tree form also makes a good subject for containers.

Roses, whether old or new varieties, bush or tree, climber or miniature, all produce beautiful blossoms in many various colors. Before selecting roses for the garden you should become aware of the various individual habits of growth, colors and compatibility with other roses and plants. Great care should be taken when combining colors with one another; an abundance of flowers and colors will not necessarily produce the gaiety one might expect, it may instead create confusion. Beauty and delight are not born of merely profuse and bright colors, rather they are brought out by the brilliance of the flowers silhouetted against a background. For this reason it is essential to remember to give thought to surroundings when planting roses, regardless of whether a formal or informal garden is planned. 🌹

Two climbing roses: 'City of York', left, and 'New Dawn', right, in Brooklyn Botanic Garden's Cranford Rose Garden.

MINIATURE ROSES IN PATIO GARDENS

HARMON SAVILLE

patio garden of miniature roses will solve the problem for those who feel they "have no space for roses." Certainly, anyone with a sunny outdoor living space such as a patio, a sundeck, a poolside area, a dooryard, a terrace or a porch has the space and the opportunity to have an exciting garden of miniature roses.

Any niche of soil that measures six inches or more across is all that is necessary to have a permanent, petite garden at the edge of patio paving, against a

HARMON SAVILLE *is the Proprietor of Nor'East Miniature Roses in Rowley, Massachusetts.*

divider or back-drop fence. If the soil is very poor, it can be removed and replaced with a mixture that is ideal for growing miniature roses. The small volume required makes it possible to "make" the soil with desirable properties: tilth, fertility and pH.

Probably the most common permanent patio garden consists of an owner-designed planter. Any contraption that will hold soil at least six inches deep can be designed to fit the patio space. Frequently, these planters take the form of "horse troughs," which are used to define the edge of an intimate living area or to outline paths for traffic flow and separate dif-

SOME MINIATURES FOR PATIO GARDENS

Every miniature-rose fancier has personal favorites. The list that follows includes the ten favorite miniatures of Stephen Scanniello, the rosarian in charge of the Brooklyn Botanic Garden's Cranford Rose Garden.

CLIMBERS

'Jeanne La Joie' — a vigorous grower with many-petaled pink flowers

'Sweet Chariot' — a good candidate for a low shrub or border with extremely fragrant mauve blooms

'Red Cascade' — a good ground cover with dark red blooms

ferent activity areas. One set of planters might outline the barbecue area with another surrounding an area furnished with chairs and tables. The planters may be raised from the ground or built up in steps. They can be made of wood, concrete or other suitable material that will fit into the patio design as an integral part of the decor. Shape and dimensions are entirely up to the individual.

For each small "micro-mini" plant, a soil volume of one-half cubic foot, (six-by-six-by-six inches), is all that is required. A full cubic foot of soil would be better for the larger size miniature plants. The only other requirements are a source of water and full sun for at least four hours (or more) per day with open shade for the balance of the day (nothing but sky overhead).

Portable Garden Features

Miniature roses are ideally suited for growing in patio pots, window boxes, planters and hanging baskets. They grow very well, very easily and produce top quality blooms. Being movable, it is possible to rotate plants in top condition to the most important areas of the living space.

Size of patio containers may be from eight inches in diameter to barrel size. The marketplace is exploding with innumerable kinds and types of containers for patio plants. Containers from eight to twelve inches in diameter are suitable for a single miniature rose. Larger planters can handle two or more plants. There is no problem in using several plants of the same variety for a large pot, but different varieties should be selected with an eye to complimentary plant habit and bloom color.

The container soil should be open and fast draining with a high humus content. A mixture of one-third good garden soil, one-third sphagnum peat moss or compost and one-third perlite will meet this requirement nicely for plastic, metal or glazed ceramic containers. An open soil is required to furnish air to the root area through the soil surface each time the pot is watered. A heavier soil (more loam and less perlite), should be used with containers of porous sidewalls such as clay, unglazed ceramics and wood. Air movement (and consequent drying) occurs partially through the sidewalls of porous pots, so it is not necessary to have such light open soil.

The most important single factor in successful patio container growing is

BUSHES

'Magic Carrousel' — a compact, bushy, red and white bi-color

'Red Flush' — a very compact, bushy plant with medium to light red very double flowers

'Rise 'n Shine' — produces brilliant clear yellow flowers on a hardy disease-proof plant

'Little Linda' — a small bush with light yellow blooms that lighten still more as they age

'Cinderella' — a micro-mini with perfectly formed light pink flowers

'Rainbow's End' — the flowers change color as they age, from yellow edged with orange to deep sunset orange and red

'Mossy Gem' — an early bloomer with flat, fragrant, magenta-colored blooms

Elvin McDonald, left, conferring with a grower at Jackson & Perkins. Miniature roses are in the pots.

proper watering. The soil must *never* dry out, even for a short period. Because of the nature of the container, the soil dries much faster than soil in the ground! You may find that your containers will need to be watered every few days when the weather is cool and damp, and daily, or several times a day, when the weather is hot and dry.

Hanging baskets need special attention because they are surrounded by drying air and because they are above eye level and can escape notice until it is too late. An automatic watering system is worth considering, especially if the "head gardener" is not on duty at all times of the day. Grouping containers closely together helps reduce evaporation and allows a longer period between waterings. A too-large container needs less watering than a too-small one.

Container plants should be fertilized frequently and lightly with a complete fertilizer that is applied as a liquid. Read the directions on the container and feed at one-half the recommended rate, twice as often. The object is to try to provide a nearly constant level of available nutrients rather than a "shot" when they get hungry.

Plant symmetry is very important in patio containers especially if they are to be viewed from all sides. Plants that are described as "compact" and "bushy" should be selected. In the event that a strong basal cane develops, the growing tip should be "soft-pinched" to help achieve symmetry and force more compact growth. The strength of the plant is thereby directed toward several smaller canes rather than a single candelabra cane.

Skillfull container growers are adept at keeping the container itself out of direct sun which results in overheating the root system. Look for ways to place the containers in the shade while allowing the plant to enjoy full light. One way this can be accomplished is to place the growing container within a large container made of solid wood or of slats. Sometimes the space between the growing pot and the outside container is filled with damp sphagnum peat to help cool and humidify and to reduce the need for more frequent waterings. ❧

REPRINTED WITH PERMISSION FROM *AMERICAN ROSE ANNUAL 1979* (AMERICAN ROSE SOCIETY).

OLD GARDEN ROSES

STEPHEN SCANNIELLO

Rosa gallica versicolor.

PHOTOS BY STEPHEN SCANNIELLO

Probably the most difficult thing about growing roses is learning all the different types. Most gardeners are familiar with the modern roses, like the long-stemmed beauties that often earn blue ribbons at flower shows. The species roses, or wild

STEPHEN SCANNIELLO *is the rosarian in charge of the Brooklyn Botanic Garden's Cranford Rose Garden. He is the co-author with Tania Bayard of* **The Roses of America** *(Holt, 1990).*

roses, are often grown for their abundant hips, an important source of vitamin C. The old garden roses are a third group of roses — a complex group ranging from the gallicas, mentioned in literature since ancient times, to the large, fragrant hybrid perpetuals, all the rage during the Victorian era. Old garden roses are the important ancestors of all the modern hybrid teas, floribundas and climbing roses.

How do you define an old garden rose? The old garden roses are all classes of roses (except the species roses) in existence before 1867. That year an historic event revolutionized the rose world. A French hybridizer, M. Guillot, combined two types of old garden roses, a tea rose and a hybrid perpetual. The result was the first hybrid tea, 'La France' — and the first of the modern roses.

There are many different kinds of old garden roses. They can be divided into eleven different classes: gallica, damask, alba, centifolia, moss, China, tea, bourbon, noisette, damask perpetual and hybrid perpetual. It's impossible to explain each of these classes in chronological order as many have uncertain origins and some seem to have evolved around the same time. However, it does make sense to divide them into two broad categories: pre-China and China-influenced old garden roses.

Pre-China Old Garden Roses

Before the China and tea roses were introduced to Europe in the 18th century, the only roses available to gardeners were types which bloom just once a season. These roses are often called the European old garden roses and consist of the gallicas, damasks, albas, centifolias and moss roses. There was an occasional repeat with one variety of damask, but otherwise all of these roses bloomed profusely during the early summer only. They were prized for their heady fragrances and became important sources of rose attar. Some of the darker-colored roses were important medicinal herbs, and gardeners were fascinated by the color range of these plants: from dark pinks and lavenders to pure white, with several varieties that are clearly striped.

The oldest known cultivated rose was a gallica, probably *R. gallica officinalis* or the 'Apothecary's Rose'. This has often been described as a red rose, but it's really a deep pink. The first lavender roses were gallicas — 'Cardinal de Richelieu' is a good example.

Both the damasks and the gallicas were cultivated by the ancient Romans and used extravagantly during their feasts and orgies. Today, damasks are impotant sources of rose oil. 'Kazanlik', a tall-growing pink damask still used as an important source of rose attar, is named for the village at the center of Bulgaria's attar-production region.

Another of the oldest old garden roses is the alba rose. It's believed that the albas are descendants of a missing hybrid of a gallica and damask rose. The name notwithstanding, albas aren't just white; there are also many shades of pink. One of the most popular is 'La Cuisse de Nymphe Emu' — translation: 'The Blushing Thigh of an Emoted Nymph'. During the Victorian era the name was changed to the more demure 'Maiden's Blush'.

Gallicas, damasks and albas were very popular throughout the early history of gardens. During the 17th century two new types of roses were discovered — the centifolias and moss roses. Centifolias were popular with the early Dutch painters and were often thought to be native to Holland, but were probably brought there from southern Europe by plant collectors. Centifolias are also known as cabbage roses because their rounded, many-petaled flowers look like cabbage heads. Centifolias are very fragrant and usually shades of pink, although some are white. Not all of the cabbage roses are large; 'Spong' and 'Rose de Meaux' are two miniature-type centifolias.

A "sport" or mutation occured with centifolias and some damask roses. These two types of old garden roses sported flowers with buds which seem to be covered with a mossy appendage. When the buds of these roses are rubbed

Jackson & Perkins®

Home Garden Excellence Since 1872

Send a friend
a J&P® catalog

The best gardening ideas have always been the ones passed along by friends and family. Just drop this card in the mail, and we'll send our catalogs to the friends you list below:

NAME

ADDRESS   APT.

CITY   STATE   ZIP

NAME

ADDRESS   APT.

CITY   STATE   ZIP

J-50A

Dept. 23X

they give off a wonderful resinous fragrance. They became known as moss roses, and with the exception of the mossy buds, they resemble their multi-petaled ancestors. Moss sports of damask roses have a stiffer, more bristlelike moss, while the sports of cabbage roses are generally softer to the touch. Mosses were among the favorite roses of Empress Josephine. In her collection at Malmaison she had one named 'Chapeau de Napoleon'.

Of all the roses mentioned so far, only a couple reliably repeat their bloom (and not very significantly at that) — the damask rose 'Autumn Damask' and the moss rose 'Salet'. This was soon to change with the arrival in the early 18th century of two new types of roses from the Far East — the Chinas and tea roses.

China-Influenced Old Garden Roses

When a small, insignificant-looking red rose was unloaded from a ship of the East India Trading Company, a tea trader named Gilbert Slater took possession of it. This rose became known as 'Slater's Crimson China'. It intrigued collectors not only because it could produce flowers all summer long, but also because of its color — true red roses had never been seen before. Similar roses began arriving from the Far East; all of them were classified as China roses. Other constant-blooming plants in exciting new colors such as apricot and pale yellow and with a more re-fined-looking bud arrived with the China roses. These were called tea roses — probably because they were packed into tea crates when they were smuggled out of China. Scholars have discovered these roses in Chinese scroll illustrations dating all the way back to 430 B.C.

The English soon began hybridizing these roses with the gallicas, damasks and other common old garden roses, with some interesting results. However, it was an accidental crossing of a damask rose and 'Old Blush', a pink China rose, on the Ile de Bourbon during the early 1800s that started a hot new trend in roses. This chance hybridization resulted in a clustered, pink, repeat-blooming flower called *R.* x *bourboniana* — the first bourbon rose.

Many different bourbon roses were collected and created by the gardeners of the famous gardens of Malmaison. One in particular — 'Souvenir de la Malmaison' — was named by a Russian baron who had wonderful memories of his visits there with Empress Josephine. Bourbon roses tend to have a globular-shaped flower and often wonderful button-eyed centers. Most of the bourbons are also extremely fragrant. 'Zephirine Drouhin' is a good specimen to clamber up a wall or over a fence, and 'Boule de Neige' has little puffy white flowers all summer long.

The noisettes were created from what appears to have been another serendipitous hybridization. In the 1760s a vigorous multiclustered pink flower was discovered by John Champneys on his rice plantation outside of Charleston, South Carolina. Philippe Noisette, a French nurseryman in Charleston, sent seeds of 'Champneys' Pink Cluster' to his brother in Paris, who became enthralled with this new type of rose with clustered, constant-blooming flowers and wonderful fragrance. He began developing new varieties. Noisette roses, as they became known, soon were the newest obsession of the rose world. With the continual influence of other old garden roses, especially tea roses, noisettes became very diversified. One large-flowered type that has a strong tea influence is 'Mme. Alfred Carierre', a beautiful climbing rose with yellow flowers with hints of apricot and pink.

However, rose enthusiasts still longed for a large flower that resembled the damasks and gallicas and repeated bloom. The teas and Chinas and their offspring were not as hardy as the other old garden roses. Plant breeders tried desperately to create an everblooming rose that would survive the damp, cold weather of northern Europe. This led to the discovery of a group known as the damask perpetuals, often referred to as Portland roses because it's thought that they descended from a rose discovered on the estate of the Duchess of Portland. This red single rose, 'Portland Rose', was probably the result of a cross between a red China rose and a bourbon. In any event, a new class evolved and they are very variable in form. Some, like 'Comte de Chambord', have large pink flowers and bloom all summer long. Others, like the magenta 'Rose de Rescht' and 'Rose du Roi', are very gallicalike in growth habit and flower color. This group of roses was an important stepping stone to the hybrid perpetuals, the rage of the Victorian era.

Bourbon rose 'Gruss an Teplitz'.

Gallica rose 'James Mason'.

In a way, hybrid perpetuals are a conglomeration of all the classes of old garden roses. The hybridizers finally created a flower that was large, fragrant and bloomed through the season. These roses didn't repeat bloom as much as the teas and bourbons. But their huge globular blooms were displayed like works of art in "English boxes" at the newly popular flower shows of the period.

It was quite fashionable for a young lady to carry a fresh cut 'Paul Neyron', with its powerful fragrance, on a Sunday afternoon stroll. And there was no higher honor for a lady than to have a rose named for her. A magenta-colored beauty, for instance, was named after Baronne Prevost, one of Empress Josephine's ladies in waiting.

However, the glorious days of the old garden rose were numbered. The historic combination in 1867 of the hybrid perpetual 'Mme. Victor Verdier' with a tea rose that gave us 'La France', the first officially recorded hybrid tea, marked the dawn of the modern rose, an era which persists to this day. 🍃

'Spong', a centifolia.

'Duchesse de Brabant', a tea rose.

HOW TO GROW OLD GARDEN ROSES

STEPHEN SCANNIELLO

GALLICAS

Rosa gallica is probably the oldest cultivated rose in existence in the West. A low, suckering shrub with large, fragrant, deep pink, crimson or dark velvety red flowers borne singly or in small clusters, *R. gallica* is a freely spreading, extremely hardy and disease-resistant rose. It can survive just about anywhere.

Each gallica has its own blooming pattern and individual flower form. Those with single or semidouble flowers produce abundant hips. Most of their blooms are on older wood, and the flowers become more profuse as the plant ages. The only pruning they need is thinning to keep them neat as old wood builds up and gets too dense. When they've grown for at least two seasons, prune them after blooming to encourage new growth for the next year's flowers. An occasional hard pruning will improve flower production.

Some of the gallicas make attractive border plants. Two of these in BBG's Cranford Rose Garden, 'La Belle Sultane' and 'Tuscany Superb', have wonderful dark green foliage. New canes climb up to six feet, while the older canes, which bear dark plum- and orange-colored hips, cascade at the base of the plants like "skirts." Needless to say, these shrubs need a lot of room. Removal of some of their older wood in the fall encourages strong, upright new canes that flower and arch over the following year.

'Complicata' can be trained as a climber — unusual for a gallica.

DAMASKS

Damask roses have very fragrant flowers that range from shades of pink to pure white and are semidouble or double. The more heavily petaled blooms tend to remain on the bush and rot; pinch them off after flowering. Damasks usually grow much larger and taller than the gallicas and have lighter-colored foliage.

Damasks need little care other than occasional thinning and removal of dead wood. After they've bloomed for two or three years, an occasional hard pruning will encourage better flower production. All pruning should be done after the flowers have faded so new growth for next year's flowers will be produced. When the canes are cut back, the laterals, or flowering stems, can be shortened by about a third. Some damasks can be pegged to the ground, which increases the production of laterals.

ALBAS

In general, albas are extremely upright, tall, hardy and easy to grow. They don't sucker easily like other old garden roses,

54

and have distinctive bluish-green leaves. Their flowers, most of which are fully double, range from white to deep pink, and they generally open wide and have good fragrance. The varieties with the fewest petals develop the best hips.

Because many albas grow very tall, they should be kept in the background in the garden. Like all the pre-China old garden roses, they don't need much pruning. Wait until they've grown for two or three years before pruning, because their best blooms are on second-year wood. As they mature some of the older wood can be removed after blooming to stimulate new growth for next season's flowers. Once in a while a hard pruning will encourage them to produce more blooms.

The taller, more vigorous albas should be allowed to attain their full height, then receive only lateral pruning and thinning; these can be trained as climbers on low fences, wrapped around pillars, or left as huge shrubs. On varieties that are more procumbent, the older wood can be cut back regularly after two or three years.

CENTIFOLIAS

Like the other pre-China old garden roses, centifolias bloom better on old than new wood. Their performance improves with age, so put off pruning until they are two or three years old, at which time any old wood that has become too dense can be cut out. It's best not to thin them too much, but an occasional hard pruning will make them produce more flowers on new growth the following season. Prune them after they've flowered. Tall-growing centifolias should be allowed to gain their full height and only have lateral pruning and thinning; if space is limited, they can be trained on pillars.

Because centifolias have foliage that is susceptible to disease, and large, many-petaled flowers that retain moisture from rain and dew, they should be planted in full sun. Otherwise they are vulnerable to black spot and mildew.

MOSS ROSES

To make the most of these roses' mossy texture, leave the unformed hips on the bush after the flowers have bloomed. Otherwise, prune moss roses in the same way as damasks and centifolias. Be sure to plant them in full sun so their flowers don't retain the evening dampness that makes them susceptible to botrytis blight.

CHINA ROSES

Chinas and their progeny tend to have more disease problems and require more care than some of the other old garden roses. China roses flower constantly on new and old growth, and therefore don't need pruning to produce new flowers. Careful pruning, however, will stimulate the best repeat blooms and improve the overall health of the plant. For maximum flower production, pinch off spent flowers to keep hips from forming.

In warm areas such as California and Texas, where they can bloom year round, China roses will thrive on neglect, growing quite large and needing only to be shaped to fit the particular growing situation or pruned to encourage new growth for flower production. If there's a moment when they're not blooming, this is the time to cut them back by about a third. In colder climates they produce their flowers more slowly during the growing season and can be pruned between period of bloom. In these areas they also have a period of dormancy during the winter, and at that time they can be pruned back by about a third to promote new growth for the next season's flowers. At the same time, remove dead and crowded wood and shape the plant.

China rose 'Old Blush'.

Hybrid perpetual 'Frau Karl Druschki'.

Damask perpetual 'Miranda'.

Chinas will do well with no pruning at all, however, no matter where they're grown. They're fairly hardy as far north as New York City, and will even grow much farther north if they're protected in winter.

TEA ROSES

The tea roses are even less hardy than the Chinas. In warm climates, they make beautiful landscape plants. During the cooler months in the north, they can be grown indoors in containers in greenhouses or under lights, then set outside as bedding plants in summer. They will die in the winter if left outside without adequate protection. All the instructions for pruning China roses apply to the tea roses as well.

A few of the hardier varieties of tea roses that survive winters at BBG's rose garden: "Mrs. Dudley Cross', which has very full, pale yellow flowers and is a

good tea rose for drier climates because the many petals don't open well in damp weather; 'Sombreuil', one of the hardiest and more fragrant tea roses and a climbing variety which can be trained on a lattice or a pillar; and 'Duchesse de Brabant', the famous rose that President Theodore Roosevelt always wore in his buttonhole.

BOURBONS

Like the Chinas, some bourbons are constantly in flower, and a certain amount of pruning will encourage abundant repeat blooms. Not all bourbons are pruned the same way, however. Basically, when a plant is two or three years old and has sufficient growth, it can be pruned while it is still dormant, at the beginning of the growing season but before that season's growth starts. The most severe pruning should be done at this time, when the main shoots are shortened by one third and all the others are shortened by two thirds. Later, after the flowers have faded, cut the laterals back again by about one third.

Some bourbons are procumbent and respond well to pegging, which produces more laterals and consequently more flowers. As the plants age, remove older wood. Other bourbons, like 'Boule de Neige', bloom freely and tend to stay shrubby, not lending themselves to pegging. If these are simply deadheaded,

56

Crested moss 'Chapeau de Napoleon'.

Bourbon roses in bloom.

Bourbon rose 'Mme. Isaac Pereire'.

they will bloom through the fall. Other bourbons do well pegged or trained as short pillars or free-form shrubs.

The bourbons are more affected by black spot than any of the other old garden roses.

NOISETTES

Noisettes need little pruning. When they are pruned, they should be treated like the China and tea roses. Some varieties, such as 'Blush Noisette' and 'Champneys' Pink Cluster', which bloom constantly, shouldn't be touched at all except to remove faded flowers and old wood. Spent flowers should simply be cut off back to the next set of leaves on the flowering canes. Vigorous noisettes like 'Mme. Alfred Carriere', which grows like a climber and can be trained on fences and posts, should be pruned like the climbers: The flower-producing lateral branches that grow off the main canes should be shortened by two thirds.

DAMASK PERPETUALS

Damask perpetuals should be pruned exactly like the damasks.

HYBRID PERPETUALS

The hybrid perpetuals are extremely hardy and well adapted to the harsh climates of many areas of the United States. They're vigorous roses that grow naturally in shrub form, producing large flowers

at the ends of their canes. To prune them, thin out older wood and cut back all the canes by about two-thirds during their dormant period. Repeat this after the first flowering.

Some hybrid perpetuals grow as climbers and can be trained on pillars. At BBG, some are also guided along a low wire to create a low hedge or border. The first year that hybrid perpetuals are pegged or trained as climbers, they will develop laterals; shorten these by two thirds after flowering. In the second and subsequent years, prune all the old laterals back by two thirds during dormancy and again after the first flowering. Peg or train all new long canes that develop.

After the first flowering period, give all hybrid perpetuals ample water and organic fertilizer, such as manure, to encourage good repeat bloom in the fall. The same should be done for all the other old garden roses as well. 🌑

ARRANGING ROSES

HERBERT E. MITCHELL

Roses don't need to be arranged. They only need to be enjoyed! The magnificent form and color of the rose make it one of the few flowers that conveys unquestioned beauty whether the composition is a single blossom or an array of brilliant color.

There are only three things you need to know about arranging roses: 1. How to care for them after they are cut. 2. Easy-to-use containers and arrangement aids. 3. A few basic floral designs that are applicable to roses.

"Post-harvest care and handling," as it is professionally identified, is everything you do from the time you cut a rose until it is placed "arranged" in some special spot to be enjoyed. So the moment you cut an emerging rose blossom, you must take off your "gardener's hat" and put on your "care and handling" hat. The manner in which you care for a rose after it has been cut determines whether or not the bud will open fully, how long it will last and how soon the color will begin to fade.

When cutting a rose, place it in a re-

HERBERT E. MITCHELL *has a management and marketing firm in Costa Mesa, California, Herb Mitchell Associates. He was President of The American Institute of Floral Designers and Managing Editor of* **Design for Profit**, *a trade publication.*

ceptacle of water as quickly as possible. If you are cutting several roses, it is a good idea to carry a container with warm water and submerge the stem in the water immediately after cutting. There are many old wives' tales about what to use to cut a rose and how to cut a stem. Use anything sharp—a knife, a pair of flower snips or pruning shears. The stem does not need to be cut at an angle. Just give it a clean, sharp cut and submerge it in water.

Make sure any containers you use to hold your rose "arrangements" are absolutely clean. Bacteria in containers are a primary cause of flower deterioration. Bacteria form quickly and are sometimes difficult to get rid of. Wash containers with warm detergent water. Use a bleach. Rinse with very hot water. If there are signs of any residue in a container, soak it in hot detergent-bleach water and use a brush to remove. Cleanliness is an absolute must in the care and handling of roses.

Use a flower preservative; roses respond very well to it. Generally, roses in a preservative solution last longer and hold their color longer than roses in plain water. The purity of your water is important too, the ideal combination being distilled water and a flower preservative. Water temperature is another factor. The

58

warmer the preservative solution—90 degrees F to 110 degrees F is best—the quicker the rose stems start absorbing.

Make sure you remove all foliage that will be below the preservative solution in the container in which you arrange your roses. Foliage under water is a main source of damaging bacteria. In fact, bacteria begin to grow almost immediately after foliage is submerged in water. As you remove the foliage and perhaps the thorns from the stem, be careful not to damage the outside layer of stem tissue.

It might sound like a lot of work to arrange roses, but it takes many hours of loving care to grow a beautiful rose blossom, so taking the necessary care and handling precautions means that your investment in growing a lovely flower will pay off with maximum enjoyment.

Ways to Arrange

There are four ways you can arrange roses. The natural way is to simply drop a blossom or a few blossoms into a tapered-neck container that will hold them in place. A bud vase, a wine decanter, a bottle or any spotlessly clean flower vase which has a pinched neck and fluted top make excellent containers for roses. Fill

BASIC SHAPES

If you want to give a professional flair to rose arrangements, you might want to follow one of the following basic shapes. In all cases, you will probably want to use saturated flower foam in the container. Floral foam holds each stem precisely where you place it.

THE EQUILATERAL TRIANGLE: One of the most popular basic forms for floral arrangements. Technically, an equilateral triangle has sides of equal length. As illustrated in the diagram, the horizontal base line of the design and the vertical height of the arrangement are equal. In constructing an equilateral arrangement, first establish the height, then the width. These two dimensions must be approximately the same length. Fill in the arrangement within the triangular form.

THE HORIZONTAL: Normally used for centerpieces. Technically, a horizontal is any shape where the total length is greater than the height. When arranging roses in a horizontal for a centerpiece, keep the height low and comfortable for conversation at the table. For coffee-table or credenza arrangements, exaggerate the height slightly. When arranging a horizontal, keep in mind how the bouquet will be used. Often people will look down into the design, therefore depth is important. To achieve a strong third dimension, bury some rose blossoms deep in the arrangement and place others throughout at varying levels.

THE VERTICAL: The perpendicular line arrangement is an excellent choice for a few rose blossoms, especially if some of the flowers are more open than others. Five or seven roses with added foliage make an outstanding vertical line design. When constructing a perpendicular, first establish the height, then add remaining flowers, keeping the vertical line tall and thin. Ideally, the width should be no greater than the width of the opening of the container.

THE CIRCLE: As a natural art form, the circle is one of the most pleasing. The "roundish" bouquet is interpreted in many ways. The "Continental," "European" and "Tussie Mussie" are some of the more popular names. The shape of the circular design is informal, but it is often difficult to construct. First establish the outside edges of the circular pattern, then fill in the shape. If you decide on a circular design, you'll want to use roses in various stages of bloom opening.

Place a cut rose in a container of water as quickly as possible. The water should be warm.

the container with warm preservative solution, remove all foliage from the part of the rose stem that will be under water, give the stem a fresh, clean cut and place it in the container. If you are using more than one stem, let each flower find a natural placement. Don't try to arrange or contrive, let it look natural; it's a great way to enjoy roses. Rather than placing one big bouquet in a single room, use a blossom or two in the rooms you use the most! And don't forget the bathroom; being greeted by a gorgeous opening rose blossom is a fine way to start any day.

If you like to use cylinder type containers you might have some difficulty making the roses stay in place. Cut a piece of chicken wire or hardware cloth about twice the width or diameter of the container. Roll it into a loose ball. Then use florist or adhesive tape crisscrossed through the chicken wire to attach it to the top of the vase. If the chicken wire shows after you have finished your arrangement, use a few pieces of shrub foliage in the arrangement to cover it.

THE RIGHT ANGLE: When constructed properly, the right angle highlights each blossom and provides the best showing for the number of flowers used. It is quite popular for modern rose arrangements. As illustrated, the height of a right-angle design should be greater than the width. The most popular, and perhaps most pleasing, right-angle arrangement flows from high left to low right. First, establish and place the height of your right-angle design at the far left of the container, then determine width. Fill in with rose blooms to create a slightly "sculptured" look as flowers are placed to connect the height with the base line.

The most important thing about arranging roses is to enjoy what you are doing. If flower arrangement is not your thing, don't worry. Simply slip some blossoms in a vase and enjoy them for what they are. If you have a flair for design, then have fun arranging your roses. The best thing about roses is that they can be enjoyed no matter how simple or elaborate the arrangement.

Pinholders are still a favorite flower holder for many flower arrangers. They are especially convenient for shallow containers or line arrangements. Contrary to many opinions, roses do not need to be in deep water to survive. An inch is ample as long as the level is kept constant and not permitted to evaporate. Place a heavy pinholder in a container, or anchor it in with clay. Trim the rose stem square and then place firmly on pinholder. When you have finished arranging the roses, add a few stems of greenery, then cover the base of the pinholder with stones.

The most popular arrangement aid is one of the floral foams. Foam is the best base to use when you want to make a centerpiece or a flower arrangement which takes on a definite shape such as a symmetrical or asymmetrical vertical composition. Before using flower arranging foam, saturate it thoroughly in warm preservative solution. Anchor it in a container by using tape across the top. Make sure you provide enough room in the container for adding water; roses need more water than a foam can provide unless there is room in the container for a constant supply of water.

After you have enjoyed your rose arrangement, remove the flowers and discard the foam. Do not reuse floral foam; very often it will not completely absorb water the second time around. This causes roses to bend their necks and wither. 🌹

A silver container displays cut roses to perfection. This one was done for BBG's annual Rose Day celebration.

EXHIBITING

IN

SHOWS

FRANK A. BENARDELLA

Exhibiting roses can be an interesting extension of your gardening hobby. The American Rose Society sponsors approximately three hundred fifty rose shows each year and most of the thirty thousand local garden clubs have sections in their shows where roses can be exhibited.

The exhibition rose (hybrid tea) by American standards should be large with abundant petalage. The petals should be symmetrically arranged with a high center. At the time of judging, the ideal bloom should be from one-half to three-fourths open. It should have good color, typical of the variety, with lots of substance. It should be clean and unmarred by moisture or spray residue. The stem and foliage must be in proportion to the

FRANK BENARDELLA *of Old Tappan, New Jersey, was President of the American Rose Society.*

bloom size. Since good foliage sets off the beauty of the bloom, it should be clean and disease-free.

To have exhibition roses one must start with varieties that can produce the type of blooms that meet the above criteria. Not all are capable of producing winners. A recent survey lists the following as being the top ten exhibition roses in the United States: 'First Prize', 'Royal Highness', 'Garden Party', 'Granada', 'Peace', 'Pascali', 'Swarthmore', 'Toro', 'Mister Lincoln', and 'White Masterpiece'. Interestingly, seven of the top ten roses are also All-America Rose Selections winners—proving that exhibition varieties can also be very good garden varieties, giving lots of color in the garden and exhibition blooms at show time. Not all perform well in all parts of the country, so check with a local American Rose Society Consulting Rosarian to see which are the best for your area.

Most exhibitors plant at least three bushes of a variety, thereby insuring bloom at show time. Planting is important to an exhibitor. Full sun is preferred and the beds are usually prepared to a depth of thirty inches, with liberal amounts of organic matter incorporated.

When the plants first leaf out in spring, a spray program to prevent insects and disease is started. Weekly applications of insecticide and fungicide keep the foliage clean and healthy. The spray program is kept up until approximately ten days prior to the show. In this way the plants are healthy, and when the blooms are cut they are clean and free from spray residue.

Fertilizing varies from exhibitor to exhibitor, but heavy feeding is the norm. Most start in early spring at the time of pruning with a cup of dry fertilizer such as 5-10-5 organic, spread around each plant. Thereafter, the plants are given a dry feeding monthly with supplements of a liquid fertilizer every two weeks in between.

The key to exhibition roses is water, for without it all the fertilizer in the world won't help the plants grow. From early spring through the growing season the plants are continually watered. Deep watering is important—a sprinkle does more harm than good. The week before the show the roses are watered almost every day. This is what gives the blooms substance, which is firmness and crispness in the petals. When roses lack water, the blooms lose color and the petals appear soft and very often droop, affecting the form.

While the roses are growing, exhibitors practice the ritual of disbudding. This is the removal of the side buds, leaving only one flower per stem. The side buds are removed so that all the energy goes into producing one very large bloom. The earlier the side buds are removed, the better. If they are removed late, telltale scars will detract from the overall beauty of the bloom.

When the roses start to come into bloom many exhibitors protect yellow and light-colored blooms from the hot rays of the sun with some sort of shade. All types of homemade "bonnets" are put over the blooms to prevent the fading of delicate varieties. Color is very important on the show table and bloom that has clarity of color will stand out against one that has been bleached by the sun.

Most rose books tell us that the best time to cut a bloom is late afternoon when the sugar content is highest. However, an exhibitor cuts his blooms when he feels they're ready to be cut, regardless of time. Usually this time is between six and ten in the morning. Once the bloom is cut, it is immediately placed in water and taken indoors where it is partially groomed. Nothing is done to the bloom at this point, but the stem and foliage are cleaned, removing all traces of spray residue. The foliage can be cleaned by rubbing it with a soft cloth moistened with a mild solution of detergent and water. No oil or other foreign matter is permitted.

When the roses have been cleaned, they are placed in a refrigerator for hardening off and storage prior to the show. Roses can be refrigerated for almost a week; however, after three or four days, they begin to deteriorate. The temperature of the refrigerator should be set as close to 33 degrees F as possible, care being taken not to freeze the blooms. Many people use paper cones around the stems during storage. These can be fashioned from freezer paper eighteen inches long. The paper is cut fifteen inches at the top and four inches at the bottom. Gluing the sides makes the cone.

'Sweet Surrender', a 1983 AARS
winner.

Modern frost-free refrigerators tend to dry out the blooms, causing loss of substance. An old-style refrigerator is preferred. If you must use a frost-free one, place waxed paper bags over the blooms, holding them on with Twistems at the base of the bloom. If you have an old-style refrigerator, it is not necessary to cover the blooms, but the humidity should be kept high. If you add a floral preservative to the water you store your roses in, you need not re-cut the stems while in storage.

Many exhibitors keep an inventory of the blooms they cut so that they know exactly what they have to work with the day of the show. Today's rose show schedules are very complex and one should read them carefully before leaving for the show. You should have an idea what classes you wish to enter, utilizing all the

roses that you cut and stored.

If the show is a short distance away, elaborate transportation methods are not necessary. Simply fill a bucket one-quarter full with cold water and place your blooms in it. Put a large bag over the entire bucket, being careful not to let the bag touch the top of the flowers. The bag is used to protect the blooms from the direct rays of the sun.

Arrive at the show early, for there is much to be done. First, find a spot in the preparation room that will be out of the main flow of traffic. It should also be well lit and free from drafts. Once you have your set-up area, obtain vases and entry tags from the show committee. Be sure the vases are filled to the top. All too often people either forget to put water in the vases or don't fill them full enough. Make a fresh half-inch cut on all stems

Roses to be shown must be carefully groomed.

before putting them in the vases.

It's now time to start the final grooming. Recheck the foliage and stem first, making sure the foliage is very clean. Remember that the rules say you can't add anything. If one leaf is badly damaged or unattractive, simply remove it. If you have a torn outer petal on a bloom, or if some of the outside petals on your red rose have white streaks in them, remove them. Work on the bloom in an attempt to arrange all the petals symmetrically around the high center. If the bloom looks lopsided (open more on one side than the other) use a Q-tip to open the tight side of the bloom, to correspond with the other side. The judges will be looking for perfect form typical of the variety.

Once the final grooming is done, put a properly filled-out entry tag on your exhibit. Some shows have placement committees, while others allow exhibitors to place their own entries. If you place your own on the table, be careful not to damage other entries. When you place your own entries you have an opportunity to observe your competition first hand. If your entry is a lot taller than the rest of the entries in the class, cut the stem to bring it down to about a half-inch above the rest. If your entry is shorter than the rest, prop it up in the vase by wedging something between the stem and vase. Do everything you can to make your entry look its best for the judge.

Exhibiting, like anything else, takes time to master. Very few people are successful on the first try, so if you win a ribbon at your first show you will probably be hooked and begin anxiously waiting for the next show to enter . . . and the next . . . and the next . . .

65

THE AMERICAN ROSE SOCIETY

HAROLD S. GOLDSTEIN

What is the American Rose Society and what purpose does it serve? The ARS was organized in 1899 to promote rose growing and to distribute cultural information on rose care. Last century's rose growers wanted more people to become involved in rose growing, but they could not possibly envision how much ARS would grow or the multitude of services in which it would become involved. The original officers, headquartered in Harrisburg, Pennsylvania, realized that a more complex organization for ARS was needed. Soon a publication evolved to help distribute rose information.

Rose societies in other cities sprang up; these societies affiliated themselves with the national organization, ARS. This trend continues and, today, there are over three hundred sixty local rose societies affiliated with ARS. Each rose society averages over one hundred members.

The American Rose Society, with its strong national membership, is among the most active plant societies in the United States, offering help, encouragement, information and social activities to its many members. Today, ARS is headquartered on one hundred eighteen acres of piney woods on the outskirts of Shreveport, Louisiana, where nearly ten thousand roses bloom annually in over thirty-five gardens. Funding for the gardens came from business firms, rose societies and individual ARS members

HAROLD S. GOLDSTEIN *was Executive Director of the American Rose Society.*

throughout the United States. Visiting the ARS gardens is an educational experience where you see how many different ways roses can be used in landscaping, both on a grand and a small scale.

An additional treat, to be viewed at the American Rose Center, is the Hybridizer's Test Garden; in this garden are grown the newest creations from rose hybridizers nationwide, including hybrid teas, floribundas, grandifloras and climbers. The roses entered in the Test Garden are judged for two years and awards are given to first, second and third place roses. One day the roses tested in the Test Garden may be introduced into commerce.

Furthermore, ARS has set up five different test gardens, located throughout the United States. One is located at the American Rose Center, where only miniature roses are grown and evaluated. The roses are entered by American hybridizers who feel that they have created a very special seedling, perhaps one worthy of commercial introduction. Miniature roses that are tested in the ARS Miniature Rose Trial Grounds and those deemed especially worthy are given the American Rose Society "E" for Excellence Award. The ARS Miniature Trial Grounds are the very first, worldwide, for the exclusive judging of miniature roses.

American Rose Society members also contribute funds which are channeled into research programs conducted by the United States Department of Agriculture, Iowa State University, Texas A & M,

Ohio State University and Oregon State, just to name a few centers of research. Topics of study include winter hardiness, rootstock, fragrance, crown-gall tumors and black-spot control. Research information, funded by ARS, is published in the *American Rose Magazine*, the *American Rose Annual* and various horticultural publications nationwide.

The *American Rose Magazine*, a thirty-two-page monthly color magazine, helps people grow better roses and keeps members in touch with rose society functions. The *American Rose Annual* averages two hundred fifteen pages and contains articles by some of the finest growers worldwide.

ARS, through its system of eighteen districts, has a program called Consulting Rosarians. Consulting Rosarians are individuals appointed by their District Director for the purpose of helping fellow rose lovers to grow better roses. A person need not be an ARS member to take advantage of these experts; one need only write to ARS headquarters. ARS will then notify a Consulting Rosarian in the appropriate area that you desire a conference or even a garden consultation.

ARS has a program by which Rose Show Judges are trained, tested and accredited. These judges must go through a training period that includes many opportunities to judge as an apprentice before actual accreditation. Once accredited, Rose Show Judges must attend periodic refresher seminars to maintain their status as active Accredited Judges.

Members of ARS are periodically surveyed to see how they rate the overall growing habits of particular roses. The information is compiled and published as the *Handbook for Selecting Roses*. Roses currently in commerce are rated numerically for interested buyers. The *Handbook for Selecting Roses* is available from ARS headquarters. Also, many nurseries purchase the handbook in bulk to distribute to their rose customers.

ARS also helps nurseries to sell their roses through marketing techniques. Local rose societies often volunteer to help rose consumers learn basic planting and horticultural practices. This advice helps the new rosarian gain years of gratification from his initial investment.

To help local rose societies maintain the interest and involvement of their members, ARS operates an extensive Lending Library and offers a wide assortment of films and slide programs. These programs help local societies present programs which are informative and educational. Also, special certificates and ribbons are available to local rose societies to use in conjunction with their rose shows and for special recognition of outstanding members.

Twice a year, the national ARS headquarters, in cooperation with a local rose society, stages a National Convention at which outstanding rosarians give programs on rose culture, hybridizing, disease control and other subject matter which is of interest to all rose growers. The exchange of ideas is an important part of rose growing.

To bring order to the vast world of roses, ARS acts as the International Registrar of Roses, registering and maintaining a permanent record of roses in commerce throughout the world. This registration system has been heralded as perhaps the finest of any floral group and has served as a model for other plant societies in their record keeping.

The American Rose Society is a great place to meet people who share your love for roses. It's also a great place to share information on growing roses. Membership information may be obtained by writing to ARS headquarters, P.O. Box 30,000, Shreveport, Louisiana 71130. ❦

THE ALL-AMERICA ROSE SELECTIONS

GEORGE E. ROSE

ll-America Rose Selections, now entering its forty-first year of public service, carries on with its program practically unchanged, controlled by carefully worded By-Laws and Rules and Regulations, much the same as those first written in 1939. The sole function of this non-profit research corporation is to carefully test the new rose hybrids entered into trials and determine which, if any, are worthy of recommendation to the buying public as being among the best roses that are to be had.

Over the years, more than two thousand new rose hybrids from all over the world have passed through two years of rigorous testing in AARS gardens. Of that number, only 109, or about 5.4 percent of those entered, have been found

GEORGE E. ROSE *was Executive Secretary of All-American Rose Selections.*

worthy of an All-America award. This indicates that AARS is functioning as it was intended to. The 1,891 entries that did not quite measure up to AARS standards have, for the most part, been kept from cluttering up the market with inferior rose varieties, to the benefit of the buying public.

This does not mean that all of the best roses are AARS award winners, nor that all AARS award winners have proven in the long run to be the best roses, but by-and-large they have consistently given satisfaction and remain the favorites of gardeners everywhere.

Maintaining a small but very active headquarters office in Shenandoah, Iowa, the AARS organization, composed of the nation's largest rose producers and hybridizers, has twenty-five official test gardens strategically located throughout the United States. These gardens are cho-

ILLUSTRATIONS BY LOTTE GUNTHART

sen to include, as far as possible, all of the soil and climatic conditions in the areas in which roses are commonly grown. The test garden locations and the official judges are chosen with great care, always with a predominance of non-member gardens and judges, to guard against any possibility of favoritism for the new introductions of member firms. In addition, member-firm judges, of which there are six out of the total of twenty-five, are not allowed to score roses entered by their companies. The nineteen non-member test gardens are located at universities or large public gardens staffed by trained horticulturists.

How Judges Score

During the two-year trial period that each rose entry must undergo, the judges are required to submit four sets of scores. Each judge must examine and score the entries for his own records as many times as possible throughout the two growing seasons. His first official spring scores must be submitted to the Secretary's office by July 1st, and his first official fall scores by November 1st. His second-year scores are submitted in the same manner, with his written comments regarding the entries included with his final two-year fall scores.

Each of the four official sets of scores is computed at the headquarters office and the results sent to all AARS members and judges to keep them informed of the progress of the entries. The computations of the two-year final scores, together with the judges' comments, are mailed to the membership at least a month before the January meeting at which the voting for award winners takes place.

According to the *Judges' Guidebook*, which is the bible of the AARS judges, there are fourteen categories on which scores for each entry are to be submitted. They are: novelty, bud form, flower form, color opening, color finishing, substance, fragrance, stem/cluster, habit, vigor/renewal, foliage, disease resistance, flowering effect and overall value.

All categories carry an equal value in that each may be scored as poor, fair, good, very good or excellent. Scoring factors of four, six, seven, eight and ten are attached to these evaluations. The values the judges apportion to the fourteen categories are then added and, by a conversion table, are converted into a numerical final score that the Secretary's office of AARS uses in computing the standing of the various entries. In order to give the judges more latitude in expressing their personal opinions of the entries gained from constantly appraising them over the period of two years, two categories (novelty and overall value) are included.

The category "novelty" may be regarded as an expression by the judge of his first impression of the entry. Quoting from the *Judges' Guidebook*: "Does it make your heart throb, or does it put you to sleep? Do you remember it in your garden, or do you have to take another look to see what was there? We want you to express this observation purposefully under novelty."

The second category is "overall value," the last category on the list. To quote again from the *Guidebook*: "Now, taking all the factors into consideration, would you plant this rose in your own garden, or recommend it to your best friend? That's really what it's all about, isn't it?"

At the January session of the membership, the two-year entry first considered for an award is the one that has received the highest score of all the two-year entries, regardless of class. The voting is carried out by secret ballot. After the ballots have been counted, the President announces whether or not the entry has been voted an award, and the action moves on to be repeated for the next highest two-year entry, provided it is of a different classification from the first one. The third entry to be voted upon is the highest scorer in the third classification, and so on, through the five classes of roses recognized by the Rules and Regulations of AARS. The cycle is repeated until the voting is closed.

The Rules and Regulations provide that there shall be a maximum limit of five varieties receiving awards in any one year. In 1951, however, no entry was considered worthy of an award, and none was given. In 1970, only one entry, which was introduced as 'First Prize', received an award. In the past forty years the average number of annual awards has been two and one half.

Entry into the AARS trials is open to any new variety from anywhere in the world that has not been offered for sale as a garden rose in this country. There is no limit to the number of roses an individual may enter, except that the entry fee increases as the quantity of entries increases. The only restriction imposed is the requirement that the entrant must be able to supply a sufficient amount of propagating stock should his entry win an award. The premise is that there would be no point in conferring an award on an outstanding rose that could not be supplied in sufficient quantity to make it available to the public within a reasonable time.

Promotion and Display

The AARS testing program would be of no value without sufficient communication to keep the public informed of the new award winners. The winners for a given year are announced in early June of the preceding year. At this time no

The locations of the twenty-five AARS Official Test Gardens are determined by population density and suitable climate.

ALL-AMERICA ROSE SELECTIONS

plants are available, nor will there be any until they appear in some fall rose mail order catalogs, with general sales following the next spring.

While this procedure may seem to be complicated, it is really not as poorly conceived as it appears. Secure in the knowledge that All-America Award winners are the outstanding roses of the country, AARS has always planned to give interested gardeners an opportunity to see each year's new award winners long before they are obtainable from any source. To make this possible, over one hundred of the largest and best public rose gardens in the country have been set up in an AARS accredited public rose garden program.

Each spring these gardens are sent a sufficient quantity of plants of the new award winners to fill an average-size bed. There is no charge to the garden for the plants which are sent under AARS number only. In June, green and white metal bed markers bearing the names of the winners are sent to the gardens and the public is invited to visit them and to see and judge the new roses for themselves. These roses will then go on sale the following fall and spring.

To keep the public advised of the new award winners, news releases describing and picturing the roses, together with information regarding the hybridizers and other pertinent facts are sent to thirteen thousand daily and weekly newspapers, selected TV stations, agricultural county agents interested in ornamental horticulture and all periodicals that would be interested in presenting the roses. These releases are accepted by the press as news and thus the service to the public for which AARS came into being completes its cycle. 🌿

THE PLEASURES AND FRUSTRATIONS OF BREEDING ROSES

J. Benjamin Williams

So you're going to hybridize roses. Good! If you're like most amateur rose breeders, you'll be very vocal and quick to say that you hybridize only for pleasure and are not interested in marketing your creations.

J. Benjamin Williams *of J. B. Williams and Associates, Horticultural Consultants in Silver Spring, Maryland, is an independent rose breeder.*

Deep down inside, I'll bet you'll dream, hope and pray for a beautiful, new, award-winning rose. Why not? It is this dream that motivates most breeders, amateur and professional alike.

Being an independent rose breeder not connected with any specific nursery has given me the opportunity to see and experience both the pleasures and the frustrations of hybridizing. Success and

Rose hips contain rose seeds.

A rose flower being prepared for pollination.

A hip forms after artificial pollination.

failure are daily occurrences for any plant breeder; if you can learn to handle the latter as well as the former, you've got it made!

How It Began for Me

My interest in rose breeding began while working in Europe after World War II, and in 1953, after much study and research, I started a breeding program. For twenty years I ate, drank and slept roses, traveled to every rose show, visited gardens and growers and read everything I could find in print. A half million crosses later, after producing and sowing some two hundred thousand seeds, I narrowed my forty-eight thousand seedlings down to two hundred fifty promising plants. Of these, fifteen have been named and registered, and ten are available for sale in this country. The most exciting moment in my rose breeding career came on a cold and snowy Sunday afternoon in January 1974 when I heard by telephone that my rose 71R75, later to be named 'Rose Parade', had won the All-America Rose Selection Award.

As a breeder and hybridizer, I know first-hand the exhilaration of playing a part in creating something new and beautiful. Creating a new rose is making a dream come true. Just to see the glistening beauty of a well-formed bud of your own plant or smell the haunting fragrance of a stately open bloom gives pleasure enough to keep one's heart young and pride enough to pop the buttons on any vest.

Rose breeding is also the people, the warmth, the friendship, the opportunity to associate with the best hybridizers in the world. It's the medium for the exchange of ideas in an area of pleasure which is not overcrowded and where the opportunity for research and new discovery is always at hand.

Expect Some Disappointments . . .

Even if you never market or plan to mar-ket your creations, you will still encounter many of the routine frustrations known to the professional hybridizer. Perhaps your seed parent will not produce hips, for not all roses are good "mothers." If "she" does produce seed, there is no guarantee that the seed will germinate. There is little, if any, statistical information on rose seed germination, and what is available varies from rose to rose and breeder to breeder. However, you can expect anywhere from 0-40 percent germination. Consider yourself lucky if you achieve twenty-five percent success.

Most professional breeders today sow their seeds directly into a greenhouse bench in specially prepared sterile media where the seeds are germinated, evaluated and finally budded out or discarded. The seedlings are never transplanted. If your greenhouse space is limited or nonexistent, you will have to transplant your new roses outdoors when weather permits, and in doing so you may be faced with the disappointment of losses due to disease, climate or unwanted visitors.

. . . and Rewards

Before long you'll feel excitement as your new plant grows and thrill as the first bud forms and opens. You'll be witnessing something no other person has ever seen. But what if the flower has too few petals, is malformed, has vegetative growth in the center, or is of poor or unstable color? What if the blooms are dull, if they blue as they age, if they burn in the sun? What if the plant is overly susceptible to disease? In all honesty, the plant should be discarded, but you should try again.

The most beautiful seedling may appear to have all the attributes of a beautiful rose while growing on its own roots the first year or two, but this same seedling may, and often does, turn into a malformed, unattractive rose when budded onto understock to be commercially reproduced. By the same token, a mediocre-looking seedling that has good blooming and growing qualities when budded onto understock for commercial purposes may turn out to be an outstanding garden rose, even an All-America Award Winner.

Follow-up

The mark of a truly expert rose breeder is the ability to recognize the value of a new rose. If you think one of your seedlings has market potential, then, by all means, pursue it. Remember, though, that even the professional sometimes suffers disappointment when one of his "best" is not introduced or accepted by the buying public.

If you send your prize seedlings to a major nursery for test, you will undoubtedly receive encouraging letters for the following two years stating that your seedlings have many outstanding qualities at times but do not have enough character or novelty to justify their commercial introduction. If you can keep from becoming discouraged and still be enthusiastic about hybridizing, every letter will bring you closer to a winner.

A professional hybridizer has to sow one hundred thousand seeds each year to market one or two new roses. The seedling must not only be new, it must also be different—and better—than anything in existence. When you're dreaming of the apple of your eye becoming a star, ponder this: there are at least twenty-five or thirty professionals in the world going after the same market that you are and who are blessed with skill, patience, attention to details, a large inventory of stock plants, good facilities and an eight-hour day. On top of that, very few seedlings make enough money to pay for the photography, patent and promotional expenses. This doesn't mean that you can't derive pleasure from your seedlings, from growing and showing them to your friends, and maybe marketing a winner.

"The Game's Afoot"

Rose breeding is a challenge, like a game of skill. Imagination, enthusiasm and perseverance make the difference between pleasure and frustration, but a few basic rules must be followed. Be a good rose grower; understand plant culture and the importance of routine care. Through study and experience, learn which roses make good parents; don't waste time on roses with bad traits or growing habits. Then, be observant, be careful, be patient, and be proud of your achievements.

If you have nerves of steel and hide as tough as leather; if you can keep your eyes open, mouth shut and smile when it hurts; if you are able to walk on glass in the presence of those with whom you must do business; if you have an unlimited source of income—then you are halfway home to becoming a successful rose breeder. If you can live with the frustrations, you'll enjoy the pleasures. May the gods bless you in all your efforts — you may need it when you start breeding roses. 🌹

N U R S E R Y
R O S E
P R O D U C T I O N

FRED EDMUNDS

All-America Rose Selection Test Garden.

Test fields at Jackson & Perkins in California.

T he production of roses in the United States stretches back into colonial times when most of the old garden roses, as we call them today, were easily propagated from slips or cuttings. When the steam vessel replaced the schooner, roses became more popular because they could be transported in winter in the dormant state from Europe, primarily England, and planted in American gardens. When World War I broke out and cut off the supply of roses from Europe, American nurserymen had to increase their production, and many of the older rose nurseries in business today date their beginnings to this period.

Roses can be grown from cuttings, but many of our most popular garden varieties are such complex hybrids that they root poorly or erratically. Grafting, particularly bud grafting, is now the most

FRED EDMUNDS *is the Proprietor of Roses by Fred Edmunds in Wilsonville, Oregon.*

common method of producing plants for sale. The only exception would be the miniature varieties whose limb structures are so tiny that it is very difficult to propagate by this means.

Rootstock and Scionwood

Initiating a crop of roses begins with a rootstock cutting. There are three major types of rootstocks produced in the United States. By far the greatest number of roses are grown on a climbing variety called 'Dr. Huey', which has the unique ability of being able to stand the irrigated desert soils of the Pacific Southwest. The combination of high salt content and high pH levels retards the growth of most understocks and yet 'Dr. Huey' survives very well and produces a fine plant. Varieties of multiflora rose, the second major type of rootstock, generally prefer cool, damp soils or acid soils and are used for production in the northern tier of states and in the rose-producing states bordering on the Gulf of Mexico. Multiflora rose can be grown in the arid Southwest, but it requires treatment to reduce the pH of the soil, and a lot more water. *Rosa* x *noisettiana* 'Manettii', the third type of rootstock, is primarily employed where the resultant plant is to be used for greenhouse forcing. It produces more and better blooms under forcing conditions for a longer period than other rootstock varieties.

The first step in field production is proper soil preparation. To insure an even rooting, the best quality, most friable soils are employed exclusively. Most fields are fumigated prior to planting to control noxious weeds and soil-borne pests that could infest the plant during the two years of intensive cultivation. Cuttings are prepared from the rootstock selected for the area. They are generally eight to nine inches in length, selected from understock blocks grown specifically to produce cuttings from long straight stems. The lower eyes on the bottom three-quarters of the cutting are removed, usually with a knife, in a process called de-eying. This drastically reduces the ability of the plant to produce suckers. The cuttings are then planted in rows from five to nine inches apart, depending upon the total amount of sunlight available. Rows average four feet apart because this matches the equipment used to cultivate and harvest. Planting is done during the dormant season, except in the northern climates where the cuttings are planted at the end of the dormant season.

Rootstock varieties are extremely vigorous, requiring only minimal amounts of fertilizer to grow. Their needs are sunshine and copious amounts of water. Many southern California fields apply as much as one hundred inches a year to keep the plants growing well and to off-set the water loss in the arid climate.

In early summer budding begins. This is accomplished by teams of two persons—one who cuts and inserts the graft, and the other who ties it firmly in place with a flat rubber budding strip that will expand to prevent girdling as the plant increases in girth. The eyes themselves are found in the axils of most leaves, and the cutting includes the bud on a shield-shaped piece of bark with a thin sliver of the woody tissue underneath. The cut made in the understock is T-shaped, and as the transverse upper cut is made, an expert budder can slightly open the two flaps of bark to allow insertion of the bud cut from the scionwood.

Scionwood comes in two forms. In former times it was cut from the previous year's budded crop growing in the field, and only those stems of approximately pencil size that and produced a bloom that had wilted and blown were considered mature enough to be used. In more recent years it has been discovered that the best budwood is taken from dormant plants in late fall or early winter, stripped of its foliage, but not the thorns, wrapped in damp newpaper, and placed in plastic bags which are held in a cool storage facility at 31 degrees F. Under these conditions the budwood will last six to nine months and produce a higher rate of bud take than will fresh wood. Within two weeks the budding can be inspected and, if an insufficient number are alive, the plants can be rebudded in a different place on the understock.

After budding, the plants continue to grow the rest of the season, storing sugars and starches in the root system to insure a superior plant the following year. In southern climates the buds can be left exposed, but in northern areas the grafts are covered with soil to prevent injury over winter. This covering also protects the buds from frost damage as they begin to sprout the following spring. Toward the end of the dormant season the tops of the understock are removed, leaving only the root system with its stored starches, plus the graft or bud that was inserted the previous summer.

In early spring the graft begins to grow, and often vigorously so. To prevent the primary stalk from breaking off, the top of the growing graft is cut back either manually or mechanically in a process known as pinching, which arrests growth and forces additional branches to arise from the graft. For the rest of the season the plant continues to grow and expand, requiring fertilizer, water and spray materials to insure that it will produce the best plant possible by harvest time.

How They Come to the Customer

Years ago roses were dug with a shovel, but modern techniques today employ a large, U-shaped blade that in one stroke cuts at a required depth and loosens the soil so that the plants are actually pulled out of the ground much as one would pull a carrot. The plants are graded with the No. 1's having three or more large canes; the medium, or 1 1/2 grade, having two or more large canes; and the small, or No. 2 plants, with two or more smaller canes. The length depends upon whether it is a hybrid tea, grandiflora, floribunda or climber, but all must have an adequate root system.

After lifting, the plants are stored in either a cool, damp, refrigerated storage, or packed in hermetically sealed containers to be shipped via refrigerated truck or rail car to storage facilities located throughout the country. A temperature of 37 degrees or less must be maintained to keep the plants completely dormant. Particular care must be taken to keep the temperature above 25 degrees to prevent injury to the root system.

The final product can reach the customer in a variety of ways. Most mail order houses and some nurseries provide bare-root plants that are shipped in hermetically sealed envelopes, then placed in corrugated cartons, to prevent drying during shipping. Some plants are root-wrapped in a moisture-holding material and placed in colorful polyethylene bags. This allows the display of the plants at local garden centers for a long period of time with little care. Should a packaged plant be purchased that has already begun to sprout, the sprouts should be removed, the plant taken from the package and placed in a hole large enough to accommodate the roots. Plants placed in larger containers extend the planting season into late spring and early summer when bare-root dormant plants would thrive only with difficulty. Some roses can be planted container and all. Others must be removed. When purchasing a container-grown plant, it's always wise to find out if the container is biodegradable or not.

Roses are extremely popular and annually nearly forty million plants reach the market, eventually winding up in someone's garden. Because a major portion of the labor involved in rose production is the hand labor that is becoming increasingly difficult to find, production methods may change as they are changing now and have changed in decades past. To insure the continuing success of roses as our favorite garden plant, commercial producers will always seek the means to grow the best possible plant at a reasonable price. ❧

ROSES OF
THE FUTURE

REPORT FROM CALIFORNIA

WILLIAM A. WARRINER

ost rose hybridizers have certain common goals although
each hybridizer should also
have aims that are nearly
unique, shared perhaps by some others
but not by all. They should continually
incorporate disease resistance, vigor and
fragrance in the selection of parents. If
these three traits are common goals,
then each breeder has his own thoughts
on other characteristics, such as ideal
plant habit, flower form and color. This
divergence of aims insures that there will
be changes in future roses and no end in
the adaptation of varieties to new uses.

In the near future, hybrid teas seem as-
sured of continued leadership in popularity. Changes in this class will occur in
color, hardiness, disease resistance and,
we hope, in floriferousness. There have
been many lavender or mauve varieties
and there will soon be some fantastic pur-
ple, plum-purple blends and variations.

Hybrid teas have been around for over
one hundred years with thousands of varieties having been introduced. Some are
better, some worse than predecessors, but

overall the breed has improved, and will
continue to improve until plants are of
ideal habit, free of disease, and bloom
continually. The blooms will be of new
colors and color patterns and will last
much longer than at present.

We have many fragrant hybrid teas,
but breeders find it very difficult to
incorporate fragrance into a large selection of varieties. 'Fragrant Cloud,'
'Granada' and 'Perfume Delight' are all
extremely fragrant but have not spawned
a profusion of sweet-smelling offspring.
'Chrysler Imperial' passed on its fragrance to 'Jadis,' but 'Jadis' has been
barren. Still, there is genetic material to
work with. Rose breeders will keep trying
for more fragrant varieties, and so those
varieties come forth.

At one period of rose evaluation, the
class called floribunda came into being
and became very popular. The blooms
were usually larger than the preceding
polyanthas and the bushes grew almost
as large as hybrid teas. It was thought, or
at least hoped, that floribundas would be
used more in home landscaping and
therefore have great popularity, but this
never proved true.

The abundant flowering of floribun-

WILLIAM A. WARRINER *is Director of Research at*
Jackson & Perkins Co. in Tustin, California.

das has made them very useful for further breeding, and many of today's floribundas carry flowers of real hybrid tea form and size with blooms in profusion. Some roses of the future will look like very large floribundas, will bloom in long- or short-stemmed clusters, and be very bushy, dense plants.

Some varieties classed as floribundas because of plant habit are really more like clustering hybrid teas, a trend that should influence the popularity of the class. If breeders can put well-formed, beautifully colored, hybrid tea-like blooms on medium high, heavily branched plants, we will have the ultimate floribunda. Or would that be the ultimate hybrid tea?

Breeding efforts of the 1970's in miniatures, ground covers, landscape types and hardy roses, plus the continuing interest in hybrid teas and floribundas, have laid the groundwork for the roses of the 1980's. There may be more confusion, however, in the minds of people who must have each variety categorized. Much overlapping exists now, but there will be far more. Roses will be available in sizes from very small miniatures, creepers and small climbers, through almost any size up to very large climbers. How can anyone then say where one classification starts and another stops?

Serious breeding for hardiness and disease control in the past decade has shown some promise for better performing roses of the future, but the surface is only scratched. If the tetraploid *Rosa rugosa* seedlings from the USDA can transmit blackspot resistance to new generations of rose varieties, then one of the big problems will have been removed. A few of the new pesticides show excellent disease control, but they still require an effort on the part of the gardener and cannot control completely.

Rose breeders are dedicated optimists and very persistent, insuring the public an ever-changing selection of new varieties. With a little luck, we will have hardy, clean, beautiful ever-blooming roses in all sizes and a new combinations of colors. 🌱

REPORT FROM NEW ZEALAND

SAM MCGREDY

I t is much easier to look into the past than into the future. In the beautiful city of Paris there is a magnificent rose garden called the *Roseraie de l'Hay*, where roses are planted in beds representing each decade. It is not difficult to see the changes which have taken place between 1920 and the present. The

SAM MCGREDY *is the Founder of Sam McGredy Roses International in Auckland, New Zealand.*

gentle grace has gone, to be replaced by the strong colors of today — the flaming oranges, the brilliant yellows, the almost coarsely healthy scarlets. Plants are stronger, colors brighter, blooms larger. Gone are the tender pinks, the subtle fragrances, the arching stems. We live in strident times, and breeders have produced roses to match.

But times change. There is a respect for our environment as never before. There is a new awareness of the importance of plants fitting into the landscape, of planting for the future, of preserving what we have.

Rose breeders are designers, the Christian Diors of the garden. They try to lead, to dictate the fashions of the future. They will probably have different ideas over the next decade. The sense of values will be evolving. I believe there will be a trend more toward breeding better plants than concentrating on new colors. To be truthful, the rose as a plant is not a pretty thing. Too often it loses its foliage in mid-season and stands there gaunt and ugly for half its length, ramrod straight, almost flowerless between flushes.

Our new roses will be much shorter in stature, with the accent on bushiness and floriferousness. They will become more truly bedding plants, competing with petunias and geraniums in the garden centers. To do this they will have to be easily and cheaply propagated, carry more flowers, need less attention, and look good over a long period. You will note that all of this has nothing to do with the commonly accepted definition of rose novelty, flower color.

These qualities will probably come from marrying the old miniature types with today's floribundas. In recent years I have seen enough exciting work with species in different nurseries to know that our plants will be quite different. To give but one example, I have seen rose types which break very freely at ground level every year. All you have to do is cut them to the ground each spring, and back they come again.

The enormous amount of money which has been plowed into the research of greenhouse forcing roses will also pay dividends for the garden. You can expect roses of much stronger petalage, well able to cope with extremes of sun and rain. The hybridization possibilities are endless. There are dozens of species roses still to contribute to our rose breeding. While I believe the accent will be on plants and plant types, there will be new colors—real chocolate browns, chocolate and lavender bicolors, unusual combinations of all types.

Oh, yes! There is an ever-increasing watch for the fragrant rose. In the coming years our roses will be more like "that old rose with the beautiful scent my grandfather used to grow." 🌹

REPORT FROM GERMANY

REIMER KORDES

As a breeder, it is a pleasure to write this article about roses of the future, and I am sure that other breeders are thinking and planning along the same lines. Some of the important points in breeding may have different priorities, but all rose

REIMER KORDES *of W. Kordes' Söhne in Elmshorn, West Germany, is a leading international rose grower.*

breeders have the same goal—better roses for tomorrow.

From our standpoint in northern Europe, hardiness is the most important characteristic. The second is freedom from diseases such as mildew, rust and blackspot. We know of so many good rose varieties which were free of mildew and other diseases when first introduced, but after some years new forms of mildew, through mutation, were able to infect these formerly resistant varieties.

Next, we look for more texture in the petals, petals which drop cleanly and, of course, free-flowering. Also, we always want as many flowers as possible, with clean and unfading colors. In recent years we have made progress in getting better-flowering hybrid teas by crossing them with floribundas. This resulted in improved flower form with larger masses of blooms.

The main consideration in breeding is still to produce new roses for special uses such as in landscaping and for planting flower borders and parks. For these purposes we need "carefree" roses, free-flowering shrub types which will give color among the green ornamental shrubs in gardens and parks. Some free-flowering shrub roses are available and are becoming popular in Europe.

There is also a need for compact forms of shorter floribundas for small-bed planting and for use in pots and containers. New shrub forms for hedges may come from *Rosa rugosa* and other species. In climbers, people prefer recurrent flowering. We still work with my father's line "kordesii," to get better ones such as 'Sympathie,' which has large flowers, nice scent and strong growth.

Hybrid teas are still the main type of rose for use in the garden and for cutting. Still, there is work enough to develop stronger plants, more flowers and the necessary lovely scent. We have developed better plants through crossing with floribundas. Other good plants should result from crossing with climbers, and with hybrid teas for bed-ding. But for this we need good, free-flowering, strong plants—floribundas, from single ones to hybrid tea forms, with keeping quality in flower and color; more use of existing ground-cover forms; carpet roses to give new ideas for use in parks and gardens.

For the cut-flower industry and for the rose lover, we have taken steps in recent years to get better keeping quality in cut-flower roses, for longer vase life. This will give the rose industry a better chance to compete with other long-lasting flowers such as carnations.

The 'Mercedes' group and 'Golden Times,' with better texture in the petals, good production under glass, and easy handling for a really good vase life, will help the commercialization of cut-flower roses. As these flowers are easy to transport over longer distances, there are greater possibilities for growing them in other and better climates, and with lower energy requirements.

Despite all the progress which has been made, the breeder still must cope with the competition from other garden plants, from perennials and summer flowers and, in the greenhouse, between roses and other cut flowers. Our attention must be to our breeding work. Rose breeders must give the rose lover better roses with more pleasure; the towns and parks, "carefree" roses; the cut-flower grower, better performance, easier handling and longer vase life.

We must look forward to make certain that the rose will keep its place as number one in the competition among plants — and remain the Queen of Flowers. ❦

PARTICULARLY ON MINIATURES

HARMON SAVILLE

Miniature rose breeding is in a dynamic and exciting phase of evolution. Breeders from all corners of the world are developing many new breeding lines. The results are dramatic improvements and a manifold increase in new varieties.

In the United States the future emphasis will be on miniatures in which the size of the flower, leaves, thorns and plant are in perfect but diminutive proportion. Given the requirements for perfect miniature proportion, the preference will be for the moderate sizes. Plant heights of 8 to 15 inches and flower diameters of 3/4 to 1 1/2 inch will best suit. The smallest miniatures, which I have called micro-minis, have less acceptance because of the difficulty in growing them and because of their diminished display value. The larger miniatures, maxi-minis, if you will, are spurned because they are "not miniatures." The main breeding thrust will therefore be in the mid-range size, with only the exceptional micro-mini or maxi-mini becoming popular.

Breeders who are working for the European market are emphasizing the display value aspect and are developing low-growing compact plants with larger flowers. They see miniatures as an extension of the very large floribunda market and visualize miniatures of the future as very low-growing plants with lots of color and ideal for bedding and container culture.

Dramatic improvements will be made in flower form. Although miniatures reflect all types of their larger counterparts there will be more and more tiny elegant flower forms featuring high centers, long pointed buds and classic hybrid tea-like shapes. Color will be available in all hues and shades, as in the large roses. The colors will be clearer and more stable with the emphasis on attractive finishing color. Fragrance will become more and more available in miniatures and will include the sweet and spicy and the damask "rose scents" that are so popular in both older and more modern roses. Foliage will become more glossy and leathery with greater resistance to disease and pest attack. And plant habits will become more compact and symmetrical.

Miniature roses lend themselves to pot culture, therefore making it possible for anyone to enjoy growing roses. They can be grown in sunrooms, on patios, on balconies, in window boxes or indoors on a sunny window or under fluorescent lighting. Miniature rose growing is within the capacity of everyone, from the elderly to the very young.

Varieties have been developed that made outstanding displays as compact, profuse-blooming pot plants. I expect these miniatures will be grown as a commercial pot plant crop to be used in gift-giving for special occasions to supplement cut roses and to be a bit more "special" than potted mums or African-violets.

All in all there should be a dramatic overall improvement in miniature roses, much like the evolution of hybrid teas and floribundas in the past thirty-or-so years. Because the genetic material is available, the changes will take much less time. 🌹

NINE FAVORITE FRAGRANT ROSES

STEPHEN SCANNIELLO

Over the years, rose hybridizers have often sacrificed fragrance for flower size and other qualities. However, few flowers can surpass the olfactory allure of a fragrant rose. Here are the ten favorite fragrant roses of Stephen Scanniello, the rosarian in charge of the Brooklyn Botanic Garden's Cranford Rose Garden.

'CURLY PINK': a hybrid tea with silvery pink blooms whose petals curl back along the edges

'ROSALYN CARTER': a hybrid tea with coral-red, long-stemmed flowers

'AMERICAN HOME': a hybrid tea with deep red blooms

'BLUE MOON': a mauve-flowered hybrid tea

'SOMBREUIL': a tea rose with large, flat, antique white blooms

'REICHSPRASIDENT VON HINDENBURG: a hybrid tea with large, silvery-pink, peony-type flowers

'FELICITE PARMENTIER: an alba with blooms in shades of pink

'LOUISE ODIER': a bourbon with bright rose-pink flowers

'MME. VICTOR VERDIER: a hybrid perpetual with large magenta blooms

Stephen Scanniello, BBG's rosarian, weeding the Cranford Rose Garden.

ESSENTIAL READING FOR ROSARIANS

DEBORAH L. KRUPCZAK

CLASSIC ROSES:
AN ILLUSTRATED ENCYCLOPEDIA AND
GROWERS MANUAL OF ROSES, SHRUB
ROSES AND CLIMBERS
by Peter Beales
Holt, Rinehart and Winston, 1985

History, cultivation and use of old roses in landscaping. Comprehensive dictionary includes information on flowers, flowering times, growth habit and cultural requirements. Lavishly illustrated with color photographs.

CLIMBING ROSES
by Christopher Warner
Globe Pequot Press, 1987

Divided into two sections: The first is on the history and cultivation of climbing roses. The second describes climbing roses — species and near relatives, old and modern climbing roses. Color photographs.

COMBINED ROSE LIST 1990
by Beverly R. Dobson

An excellent reference on sources of roses and updates on rose registrations. Available by mail order only. For more information, write Beverly R. Dobson, 215 Harriman Road, Irvington, NY 10533.

DEBORAH L. KRUPCZAK *is a horticulturist who works as an information specialist in the Brooklyn Botanic Garden library.*

THE COMPANION TO ROSES
by John Fisher
Salem House Publishers, 1987

An encyclopedia of places, people and stories relating to roses. Delightful reading, it explains the origin of many terms in the rosarian's vocabulary. Color and black and white illustrations are scattered throughout the text.

THE COMPLETE BOOK OF ROSES
by Gerd Krussmann
Timber Press, 1981

Rose history, cultivation, reproduction and hybridization, along with descriptions and classification of the genus Rosa. Line drawings, some black and white photographs.

THE DICTIONARY OF ROSES IN COLOR
by S. Millar Gault & Patrick M. Synge
Published in collaboration with
The Royal Horticultural Society and
The Royal National Rose Society.
Mermaid Books, 1971

Includes a short description of each rose and over 500 color plates. Black and white photographs illustrate pruning and propagation techniques.

A GARDEN OF ROSES
by Graham Stuart Thomas
Salem House, 1987

Descriptive text, including historical notes, accompanies exceptional watercolor illustrations of roses.

THE HERITAGE OF THE ROSE
by David Austin
Antique Collectors' Club Ltd., 1988

Descriptions of rose hybrids and species, with chapters on using roses in the garden and on cultivation. More than 300 color illustrations.

HISTORY OF THE ROSE
by Roy E. Shepherd.
The Macmillan Company, 1954

History of the different groups of roses based on their first recorded mention, with descriptions of plants in each group. Black and white photographs.

MODERN ROSES 9
P.A. Haring, Editor
The American Rose Society, 1986

The international checklist of roses in cultivation or of historical or botanical importance.

OLD ROSES
by Mrs. Frederick Love Keays
The Macmillan Company, 1935

Good information on roses developed before 1880 written in an informal, chatty manner. Descriptions of roses are grouped by time period. A few black and white photographs. Hard to find, but worth a trip to the library or old book store.

THE OLD SHRUB ROSES
by Graham Stuart Thomas
Phoenix House, 1965

The development and cultivation of old roses. Black and white and color photographs.

PETER MALINS' ROSE BOOK
by Peter Malins and M.M. Graff
Dodd, Mead & Company, 1979

Written by the former rosarian of Brooklyn Botanic Garden's Cranford Rose Garden, it includes information on growing roses as well as critical evaluations of specific roses.

ROSES
by Gertrude Jekyll and Edward Mawley
Introduced and revised
by Graham Stuart Thomas
The Ayer Company, 1983

Originally published in 1902 as Roses for English Gardens, this is a classic for every rosarian's library. Black and white illustrations primarily, with a few color photographs.

ROSES
by Jack Harkness
J.M. Dent & Sons Ltd., 1978

Describes how roses are grown and hybridized. Descriptions and evaluations of species for subgenera and hybrids.

ROSES OF AMERICA:
THE BROOKLYN BOTANIC GARDEN
GUIDE TO OUR NATIONAL FLOWER
by Stephen Scanniello and
Tania Bayard
Henry Holt, 1990

A comprehensive look at roses in America, from the old garden roses through the most recent varieties, concentrating on the hundreds of roses at BBG's Cranford Rose Garden. Lots of practical tips on growing roses. Scores of color photos.

SHRUB ROSES OF TODAY
by Graham Stuart Thomas
J.M. Dent & Sons Ltd., 1980

Descriptions of shrub roses with a key to the major groups of cultivated roses. Includes an interesting section on fragrance. Some black and white illustrations.

TWENTIETH-CENTURY ROSES
by Peter Beales
Harper & Row Publishers, 1988

A discussion of the different types of modern roses, including cultivation and plant descriptions. Color photographs.